mr. sunday's saturday night chicken

mr. sunday's saturday night chicken

LORRAINE WALLACE

Food Photography by Alexandra Grablewski
Cover Photography by Nancy Ellison

WILEY

John Wiley & Sons, Inc.

Food photography copyright © 2012 by
Alexandra Grablewski
Food styling by Brian Preston-Campbell
Prop styling by Martha Bernabe

Published by John Wiley & Sons, Inc.,
Hoboken, New Jersey.

Published simultaneously in Canada.

For general information on our other products
and services, or technical support, please contact
our Customer Care Department within the United
States at 800–762–2974, outside the United States
at 317–572–3993 or fax 317–572–4002.

Wiley publishes in a variety of print and electronic
formats and by print-on-demand. Some material
included with standard print versions of this
book may not be included in e-books or in print-
on-demand. If this book refers to media such as
a CD or DVD that is not included in the version
you purchased, you may download this material
at http://booksupport.wiley.com. For more
information about Wiley products, visit www.
wiley.com.

Library of Congress Cataloging-in-Publication
Data:

Wallace, Lorraine.
  Mr. Sunday's Saturday night chicken / Lorraine
Wallace.
     pages cm
  Includes index.
   ISBN 978-1-118-17530-9 (pbk.); ISBN 978-1-118-
29749-0 (ebk); ISBN 978-1-118-29755-1 (ebk); ISBN
978-1-118-29765-0 (ebk)
 1. Cooking (Chicken) I. Title. II. Title: Mister
Sunday's Saturday night chicken.
  TX750.5.C45W35 2012
  641.6'65--dc23

                                       2011051094

Printed in the United States of America

10 9 8 7 6 5 4 3 2 1

To
Mr. Sunday
and our
beautiful family

Contents

Acknowledgments   11
Introduction   13
The Keys to Using This Book   18
Chicken 101   19

Fall   31

Rotisserie Chicken à la King   34
Martin's Chicken Marsala   35
Tandoori Roast Chicken   36
Chicken Marengo   38
Chicken with Angel Hair Pasta and Rosemary Sauce   39
Quick Chicken Stir-Fry   41
Classic Chicken Pot Pie   42
Sausage Pasta Rustica   45
Turkey Meatballs with Spaghetti Squash   47
Honey-Mustard Chicken with Apples   48
Chicken Scaloppine with Pears   49
Thin-Cut Chicken Parmesan   50
Turkey or Chicken Tetrazzini   51
Country Chicken-and-Mushroom Fricassee   52
Wagshal's Famous Roasted Hormone-Free Chicken   53
Chicken Enchiladas   54
Skoda's Braised Chicken with Mushrooms and Cashews   56

Winter   59

Polenta Gratin with Turkey Bolognese   62
Coq au Vin   63
Half-Hour Chicken and Leek Stew   64
Chantima's Herb-Roasted Chicken with Vegetable Gravy   65
Crispy Pan-Roasted Chicken with Garlic-Thyme Butter   66
Individual Winter Vegetable and Chicken Pot Pies   68
Turkey Meat Loaf with Home-Style Gravy   70
Stovetop Chicken Cacciatore   71

Balsamic Butterflied Chicken with Roasted Vegetables   73
Turkey Burgers with Pimiento Spread   74
Al Tiramisu Tuscan Duck Stew   76
Holiday Lemon Chicken   77
Chicken in a Pot   78
Citrus-Chili Cornish Hens with Lemon Sauce   80
Indian Butter Chicken   82
Nancy's Braised Chicken in Orange Juice   83

Spring

   85

Quick Turkey and Green Bean Stir-Fry   87
Spring Chicken Roll-Ups with Lemon Sauce   88
Quick Chicken Cordon Bleu   89
Fajita Chicken Packets   90
Red Curry Chicken with Vegetables   91
Spring Chicken with Artichokes and Fennel   92
Ida's Baked Chicken   93
Pantry Chicken Saté with Peanut Sauce   94
Chicken Scaloppine with Sugar Snap Peas, Asparagus, and Lemon Salad   96
Chicken and Cashews in Lettuce Cups   99
Sesame Chicken with Edamame   100
Greek Stuffed Chicken Breasts   101
Art and Soul Fried Chicken   102
Quick Chicken and Vegetable Quiche   105
Low-Fat Chicken Tagine with Parsnip Puree   106

Summer

   109

Basted Barbecue Chicken with Carolina-Style Barbecue Sauce   112
Sautéed Chicken and Zucchini with Tarragon Pan Sauce   114
Grilled Pesto Chicken   115
Creamy Chicken Salad   117
Herbed Buttermilk "Not-Fried" Chicken   118
Oven-Grilled Chicken with Roasted Grape Tomatoes   119
Stovetop Summer Chicken   120
Skewers of Sage Chicken with Sweet Italian Sausage   123
Butterflied Grilled Chicken with Ginger-Citrus Marinade   124
Grilled Chicken and Herbed Farfalle Pasta Salad   126
Grilled Chicken Paillards   127
Chicken Kebabs with Creamy Pesto Sauce   128
Southern Oven "Unfried" Chicken   129

Friends and Family 131

Ann's Hot Chicken Salad Pie 136
Newnam's Chicken Tacos with Anna's Secret Guacamole 138
Monahan Family's Jerk Chicken 141
Bonnie's Curry Chicken Salad 142
Peter's Beer Can Chicken 144
Nana's "No Peek" Chicken 145
Sharon's Asian Chicken Salad 146
Ann's Texas Fried Chicken 147
Pauline's Easy Roast Chicken 149
Robin's Mediterranean Chicken 150
Patty's Roasted Chicken 151
Diana's Quick Chicken Divan 152
Liz's Chicken Kiev 153
Grace's Dad's Chicken 155

Two-By-Two Dinners 157

Chicken Saltimbocca with Quick Lemon Sauce 158
Chicken Dijonnaise 160
Chicken Wallace Quick Skillet Dinner 161
Sesame Chicken 163
Chicken Fajitas 164
Chicken Piccata 166
Herbed-Breaded Chicken Tenders with Orange Marmalade Mustard 167
Dill Havarti–Stuffed Chicken Breasts 168
Chicken and Soba Noodles One-Dish Dinner 169
Chicken Cutlets alla Pizzaiola 170
Baja Chicken with Warm Mango Salsa 171
Chinese Chicken and Mushrooms 172

Game Day 175

Mexican Chicken Casserole 178
Shredded Turkey in a Bag 179
Wings Three Ways: *Sweet-and-Sour Chicken Wings with Peanut Dipping Sauce; Teriyaki Chicken Wings with Spicy Citrus Sauce; Buffalo-Style Chicken Wings with Light Ranch Dressing* 180
Caribbean-Style Chicken 184
Panko-Crusted, Blue Cheese–Stuffed Chicken with Buffalo Sauce 185
Chicken Teriyaki 187
Karl's Two Kinds of Texas Quail 188
Diane's Tennessee Quail 189
Ayrshire Farm's Brined Organic Pheasant 190
Swiss Embassy Roast Turkey 191

Smoked Orange Duck 192
Remick's Hot Sauce Tacos 193
Turkey Gobbler Sandwich 194
Dickens' Christmas Goose 196
Dan's Chicken Cheeseburger Slider Salad 197

Sides 199

Asian Noodles 200
Baked Brown Rice 201
French Lentils 201
Black-Eyed Pea Salad 202
Classic Mashed Potatoes 204
Classic Moroccan Couscous Salad 205
Baked Brussels Sprouts 207
Sautéed Red Cabbage 207
Corn Salad 208
Creamy Cheesy Grits 209
Easy Baked Beans 210
Fried Okra 211
Vinegar Slaw 212
Herbed Potato Bread Stuffing 213
Gruyère Cheese au Gratin Potatoes 214
Greek-Style Lima Beans 216
Grilled Romaine Salad with Creamy Ranch Dressing 216
Grilled Tomatoes 217
Jasmine Rice 217
Individual Corn Puddings 219
Kale Crisps 220
Lemon Orzo 222
Mushy Peas 222
Panko Green Beans with Slivered Almonds 223
Pan-Roasted Herbed Fingerling Potatoes 225
Parsnip Puree 226
Pickled Cucumbers 227
Sweet Potato Wedges 227
Picnic Potato Salad 228
Southwest Chopped Salad 229
Spinach and Mushroom Sauté 230
Spinach Salad 231
Stuffed Tomatoes with Cucumbers and Feta 232
Sweet-and-Sour Spring Carrots 232
Vineyard Quinoa Salad 235

Acknowledgments

I am grateful to the many dedicated and talented people who helped make this book possible.

Thank you:

My husband Chris and our children—Peter, Megan, Catherine, Andrew, Sarah, and Remick—for the love and encouragement that they give me unconditionally.

Mom, for teaching me to always use organic ingredients, and how to cook.

My family, for both recipes and memories: Mike and Mary Wallace, Kappy Leonard, Pauline and Richard Bourgeois, Jennifer Wallace, and new son in-law Miguel Calderon, and baby Sabine Calderon Wallace.

My friends: the Frees, Jefferys, Monahans, Bonnie McElveen-Hunter, Caseys, Ann Hand, Newnams, Musses, Warrenders, Dubins, Benders, Smiths, Gildenhorns, Karl Rove, and the Sukas for sharing their favorite chicken dishes.

Chef Art Smith of Art & Soul and Lyfe Kitchen restaurants, Frank Pelligrino of Rao's, Chef Billy Martin of Martin's Tavern, Chef Luigi of Al Tiramisu, Chef Ann Marie of Wagshal's market, Larry La of MeiWah, and Chef Rob Townsend for giving me recipes for chicken and inspiring me.

Sandy Lerner for showing us her Ayrshire Farm and teaching us the blueprint for organic farming. Vicki Bendure, of Bendure Communications, for her encouragement and support.

My agent Michael Psaltis of the Culinary Entertainment Agency, who always helps me with the details and never lets me lose sight of the big picture.

Dan Macy, of dantasticfood, Inc., for his friendship and culinary artistry in styling, tasting, testing, and writing.

My editor, Justin Schwartz, for his vision and professionalism.

My publisher, John Wiley & Sons, for believing in me and making my vision come true with all of their hard work.

Cover photographer Nancy Ellison, for being such a dear friend and sharing her keen eye for photography.

Katy Ricalde, Ashley Wainer, Flip Bowery, and Kathy Campenella for their Web site support and designs.

11

Introduction

Nine years ago my husband, Chris Wallace, accepted a position at Fox News as the anchor of its political talk show, *Fox News Sunday*. This decision turned our family life upside down, especially our weekend routine. Suddenly, Saturday nights were a time to get to bed early, not to go out. And keeping our household quiet was a new experience because we still had teenagers at home with hectic sports and social schedules, especially on weekends. This is also about the time that I became interested in expanding my knowledge of food. Or you might say I became a food enthusiast. Now, on Saturdays my kitchen is always like a science lab: a pot of soup is bubbling on the stovetop for our "Soup Sunday" lunch the next day, and new recipes are being created and tested. I always get a great sense of satisfaction when my family gives a new recipe a "Thumbs-Up!"

But while I create new dishes all the time, I have to deal with a husband who likes to say, "Change is overrated." Chris has been known to buy a new suit and keep it in his closet for a month before he will start wearing it. His favorite meal is chicken. It's his comfort food. And after I served him chicken the first few Saturday nights before his show, he said "Let's stick with chicken." So chicken became, and still is, our Saturday night dinner. Just like our Soup Sunday tradition that inspired my first book, our Saturday night chicken has become a family ritual. After roasting just so many chickens, though, I decided to get more creative and explore new ways of cooking and preparing chicken. In this book, you will find more than one hundred handy recipes, accompanied by thirty-five delicious sides that I prepare to gather my family around the table.

No other food seems to provide the same kind of dinner insurance. A chicken in the fridge can guarantee at least one good dinner, and often two. Chicken is among the most versatile of food items, and one that is inspiring for the beginner and well-seasoned cook alike. It is not only great for economical, quick-fix dinners, but also for special occasions; for guests at home or for take-away picnics; served hot or cold. And it is even better the second day as leftovers for lunch or dinner.

Chicken offers endless variety. It can be quick and easy to prepare, and there is a chicken dish for every season, mood, or occasion. Each recipe in the book has a family story, or comes from a chef, place, or friend that we hold dear to us. There are many beautiful pictures of the finished dishes to show how best to prepare the recipe—as well as some photos I share from our family album—and some fun facts throughout to expand your knowledge of chicken.

Shopping at the Home Farm organic market, Middleburg, Virginia

LORRAINE WALLACE
AUTHOR, MR. SUNDAY SOUPS

top left: Chris and Lorraine in their garden, photo by Nancy Ellison.
top right: On my first Satellite tour with Mr. Sunday himself!
left: Megan and baby Sabine watching dad

In the section Chicken 101 (page 19), I explain some of the terminology used by the poultry industry to help you select the best product in the farmers' markets or at grocery stores to feed your family well. I'll also give you some cooking tips about how to debone, butterfly, roast, and carve chicken, along with the safest temperatures for preparing the perfect bird.

The Washington area is home to some special chicken and organic farms, like Ayrshire Farm in Upperville, Virginia. I will introduce you to the people I've met at this beautiful farm, who are dedicated to bringing us this perfect food source. People worldwide are questioning our dependency on processed foods. As a result, they are returning to locally grown foods, encouraging cooking that uses seasonal ingredients, and preparing healthier food for their families. Luckily, these trends and local ingredients make for the best dishes! I'll share with you what I've learned about my local farms and explain how you, too, can incorporate this knowledge and approach in your cooking.

In *Mr. Sunday's Saturday Night Chicken*, there are chapters for each season. I look forward to the change of seasons and the new, fresh ingredients each brings. For instance, in the "Fall" chapter, I show you how I prepare Chicken Scaloppine with Pears. This dish is light, but bursting with the sweetness of this autumn fruit.

Chris and I like to go to the movies on his Mondays off from work, and afterward go for a "date night" to Martin's Tavern, a Washington landmark. Chef and proprietor Billy Martin shares his delicious Chicken Marsala, just brimming with fresh mushrooms and a brown sauce you wipe off the plate with warm homemade bread.

As the weather gets crisper, I look forward to the smell and warmth of the kitchen when I roast a chicken with lots of fresh herbs and vegetables. After roasting a chicken, I like to make a classic pot pie to create a meal from the leftovers.

Chef Luigi Diotaiuti, owner of Al Tiramisu restaurant here in Washington, shares his delicious winter classic, Tuscan Duck Stew, which he prepares two ways— for a casual or a fine-dining meal. In the "Winter" chapter, I

top: Andrew, Megan, and Catherine.
above: Ayrshire Farm heritage turkey, Upperville, Virginia

also make a classic Coq au Vin that I prepare on the stovetop.

As you can imagine, the chicken recipes I make in the "Spring" chapter are lighter and use many fresh vegetables from the early crops and promises of warmer weather. One of my favorites is Chicken Scaloppine with Sugar Snap Peas, Asparagus, and Lemon Salad. You simply pound a chicken breast until thin and quickly sauté it, then serve it with steamed fresh sugar snap peas and asparagus, dressed with a lemon vinaigrette, and a final hit of fresh mint. It is a great start to the abundance of the season.

As the weather gets warmer, who doesn't like the smell of the barbecue and the

The Peter Wallace family: James, Jennifer, William, Caroline, Peter. Photo by Libby Bourne.

taste of grilled chicken? In the "Summer" chapter, there are recipes for cooking outdoors and for achieving the same flavors indoors. My daughter recently informed me that National Fried Chicken day is July 6. I share with you my mother's healthier version: Herbed Buttermilk "Not-Fried" Chicken, which you bake in the oven. Renowned chef Art Smith shares with us his Southern Oven "Unfried" Chicken, which is his signature dish at Lyfe Kitchen in Palo Alto, California, as well as his famous Art and Soul Fried Chicken from his restaurant here in Washington.

In the "Friends and Family" chapter, you'll find a variety of recipes gathered from our dear family and friends. The cherished recipes in this chapter are from the likes of our children's godparents and school friends to new and old neighbors—the rope holders in our lives who bring us so much joy and love. What a thrill it is for me to be able to share and pass on these special recipes. Keep the recipe donations coming, my dear family and friends!

The "Game Day" chapter features recipes for entertaining on those days when we all gather around the television to watch sporting events. Many of these recipes can be prepared ahead of time, so you can kick back and enjoy the games. For instance, my Mexican Chicken Casserole is a feisty one-dish meal, easy to prepare in advance and then warm when ready to eat, and serve with a Southwest Chopped Salad (see "Sides"

Remick, Catherine, Chris, Kappy, me, Andrew, and Sarah, Thanksgiving 2010. Photo by Michael Bennett Kress.

chapter). Or try my friend Dan's Chicken Cheeseburger Slider Salad, a meaty crowd-pleaser. So keep your game face on and enjoy your day around the television or out in the fields cheering on your favorite team.

Also featured in this chapter are the birds that are often cooked for the holidays or special occasions—like the Thanksgiving recipe from the wife of a former ambassador to Switzerland, which was served at the embassy in Geneva. Then there are recipes for quail, pheasant, and Christmas goose to make your holidays special.

Another feature of *Mr. Sunday's Saturday Night Chicken* is a chapter called "Two-By-Two Dinners," which shows you how to prepare two chicken breasts or cutlets with few ingredients in a short amount of time. I was urged to add this chapter by our children, who are young working adults and on budgets both for time and money. Lastly, the "Sides" chapter offers some of the Wallace favorites our family enjoys for all the seasons, occasions, and fun times around the table.

So whether you are looking for time-saving recipes, quick suppers, or inspiring new ideas for roasted chickens, salads, pasta, or festive special occasions, *Mr. Sunday's Saturday Night Chicken* rules the roost!

The Keys to Using This Book

I've placed icons on many of the recipes so that you can tell at a quick glance whether the recipe fits your needs and schedule. The keys to the icons are:

$: These recipes use whole chickens, which is the most economical way to buy chicken. While some recipes require simply cooking it whole, others may instruct you to cut the chicken into pieces. See Chicken 101 (next page) for specific instructions. Economical recipes in the Sides chapter are also marked with this icon.

BONELESS, SKINLESS: Recipes here are made with boneless, skinless chicken breasts, which are generally quick and easy to prepare.

QUICK: All the recipes can be prepared in 30 minutes or less.

ROTISSERIE CHICKEN: Store-bought rotisserie chickens are used in these recipes with most requiring the meat to be pulled and shredded—much easier and quicker than boiling or roasting an entire chicken yourself.

GOOD FOR COMPANY: The recipes here make enough for a crowd and some are perfect for elegant entertaining.

POTLUCK: These recipes are great to make ahead and bring to a potluck-type event.

STOVETOP: The entire recipe can be made on your stovetop and doesn't require heating up your oven.

FAMILY FAVORITE: These recipes are ideal for weeknight family meals and are a favorite in my house.

ONE POT: The recipes require the use of only one pot or pan to create an entire dish.

VEGGIE: Eliminate the chicken for a vegetarian dish.

GRILL: The recipes are prepared on an outdoor gas or charcoal grill.

COOK'S NOTE: I am not a trained chef but have made dinner for a blended family nearly every night for decades. One of the things I've learned over the years is that recipes should be considered as meal ideas and as guidelines. It's no use driving yourself crazy running to the store when the recipe calls for a red bell pepper and all you have is a green bell pepper.

Feel free to improvise and make my recipes your recipes. The meals in this book have been created for my family by tinkering with the ingredients based on what I had on hand, the preferences of my family, and plenty of input on how to make them even better. I hope you and your family make them your own.

Chicken 101

Someone once said that chicken is to a cook what canvas is to a painter. It is served to us boiled, roasted, fried, hot or cold, whole or in pieces, with or without sauces, boned, skinned, stuffed—and always with equal success. The chicken has become part of nearly every cuisine around the world and made easier to cook with so many different cuts now available in most markets. The boneless, skinless breast has become the staple for most American family weeknight dinners and now, the more flavorful boneless thigh is also easily found as well. But buying chicken can be confusing, because of all the various terms used to describe the process by which the birds are raised, processed, and sold. Below are definitions of the terms that you will often see in the market and advice on how to select the right bird for your needs.

HOW TO SELECT A GOOD BIRD

Good birds should be pink. Stay away from any chicken that has grayish meat or has a transparent looking skin since that can signal that the bird may have been sitting around in a freezer too long. Examine the skin for any tears or signs of rough handling. Damaged skin and meat tend to deteriorate quickly. Check for a "sell by" date on the package. Also avoid purchasing chicken with any packaging that has accumulated a lot of blood—often an indication that it may have been handled a bit roughly in transit. Look for chicken labeled as organic, grass-fed, heritage, antibiotic-free, certified humane, and properly raised local types. Not only will you feel better about buying these birds that are raised humanely, you'll appreciate how much better these chickens taste.

Also, don't hesitate to bring the chicken up to your nose and take a whiff. Fresh chicken should have no smell. Once you get home, immediately place it in the refrigerator for up to two days. If you plan to use it later than that, place it or the portions in a freezer bag and label with the date of purchase. It's also helpful to label what's inside (i.e., drumsticks or boneless, skinless breasts). Often, chicken pieces can all look the same once frozen. Chicken can be frozen for up to three months.

HOW MUCH TO BUY

One broiler-fryer—2 to 3 pounds—cut up, yields enough servings for four people. A roaster chicken—3 to 6 pounds—can be enough for up to eight people. One whole chicken breast or two chicken breasts halves—about 12 ounces—generally serves two people. One pound of chicken thighs, drumsticks, or even wings can serve two people as well.

TERMS TO KNOW

ORGANIC: The United States Department of Agriculture (USDA) defines organic as chickens that are raised without antibiotics and fed only organic feed that is free of synthetic fertilizers and pesticides. The USDA prohibits the use of the term *organic* on packaging of any food product not produced in accordance with its rules.

GRASS-FED OR PASTURE-RAISED: The birds are raised on low-fat diets of fresh grasses, eating on their own schedules and spending much of the time outdoors. Generally, grass-fed chickens cook a bit faster since they are leaner.

FRESH: Use of the word *fresh* on a label indicates that the product has never been frozen or chilled below 26°F.

LOCAL: Chickens are generally raised at a farm that is close to where you're purchasing it. The product has traveled a shorter distance from farm to table, therefore using minimal fossil fuels. The chicken supports the link between the local farmer, consumer, economy, and the environment, thus fostering communities. The local chicken is likely to have been raised responsibly. It may or may not be certified organic, but often small, local farmers follow organic practices.

HERITAGE BREEDS: The term refers to poultry breeds that were raised in the days before industrial agriculture reduced the breed variety. These breeds are sustainably raised, which means with the best practices for the animal, the community, and the environment. The heritage breeds are generally firmer, juicier, and more flavorful since they aren't fattened and rushed to market.

KOSHER: Kosher chickens are raised and slaughtered according to Jewish dietary regulations. The birds are hand-salted during the processing and therefore the meat is saltier than non-kosher birds.

AIR-CHILLED: This poultry undergoes a process using cold air instead of water to chill them. The air-chilled process is used in Europe and Canada but is relatively new to the United States. One brand name you might recognize that uses this process is Bell & Evans.

RETAINED WATER: Often you may see a package labeled "may contain up to 6 percent retained water," which means the chickens are chilled in ice water after processing with the retained water amount listed on the label. The process retards the growth of spoilage bacteria and other microorganisms.

WHAT TO WATCH OUT FOR

ENHANCED: This means that a solution, often water and salt, has been used to flavor and tenderize the bird. Sometimes chicken broth is injected into the bird. The solutions can increase the weight of the bird, which means that you end up paying more for the same amount of meat. Processors that make enhanced products suggest it provides a more tender and consistent product that is more reliably moist when cooked. But if you properly cook your bird, you won't have to worry about starting with an "enhanced" product.

NATURAL: This means the chicken feed does not contain any artificial ingredients, coloring, or chemicals and is minimally processed. Sometimes birds labeled natural are still treated with artificial hormones or are injected with a salt solution or processed flavors.

FREE-RANGE: In recent years, more and more farmers have started raising small flocks of free-range chickens. With diets consisting mostly of insects and grass, they are much more flavorful. While the term suggests that the bird had access to natural grass and was living outdoors, it does not have to be certified by the USDA. Chickens may be labeled "free-range" if they were given some access to the outdoors. That doesn't mean that the chickens were raised in a large grassy area in which to roam. This could simply mean that the chickens were given access to a fenced area filled with dirt.

HORMONE-FREE: This is often an empty claim since federal laws prohibit any commercial grower from adding hormones or steroids to chicken products.

FARM-RAISED: All chickens are raised on farms—commercial or private. So the label "farm-raised" can refer to any chicken. This term is often used on restaurant menus, but in such usage it usually refers to a locally raised chicken.

CAGE-FREE: While it sounds nice, the birds can still be raised in tightly packed sheds without much room to move and without access to the outdoors or clean surroundings.

A WORD ABOUT SAFE HANDLING

When handling raw chicken, it is best to keep everything that it comes into contact with clean. You will note that most of my recipes begin with the language "rinse the chicken with cold water and pat dry with paper towels." Your hands, the sink, work surfaces, cutting boards, and knives or poultry shears should all be washed with hot soapy water after working with raw chicken. Any sponges that have been used to clean up any chicken juice should be thrown into the dishwasher or rinsed thoroughly in hot soapy water. Raw chicken can harbor salmonella bacteria. If bacteria is transferred to work surfaces or utensils, they could cross contaminate other foods. So, it is always best to play it safe.

As with any perishable meat, bacteria can be found on raw or uncooked chicken or other poultry, so safe preparation is crucial. Bacteria begin to multiply between the temperatures of 40°F and 140°F, which is the temperature range your chicken will likely be after you remove it from the refrigerator and when you are prepping it. So, this is the most crucial time for safety.

The USDA's Food Safety and Inspection Service recommends dedicating a specific cutting board just for meat. Many retailers sell multicolored cutting boards that can be dedicated just to chicken. There is some research that wood cutting boards actually limit bacterial growth. Whether you use plastic or wood, be sure to thoroughly clean your board in hot soapy water after use.

Cooking Tips

DISJOINTING A BIRD

Poultry pieces purchased from grocery stores are sometimes poorly trimmed and, pound for pound, are more expensive than a whole chicken. By learning how to cut poultry at home, you can save money. And the added bonus is the special bag of giblets found inside of the chicken cavity, which makes an easy and flavorful gravy.

To disjoint a chicken, you will need a cutting board with a damp cloth or paper towel underneath to prevent slippage, a sharp chef's knife, and a confident hand. Learn to locate the joints of the chicken by feel so that, when you bear down with a knife, you

avoid the bones and cut through at a point of least resistance, meaning just tendons and cartilage.

To start, place the chicken, breast side up, on a cutting board. Remove the leg portions first. Pull one leg away from the body and cut through the skin between the thigh and body on both sides. Then bend the whole leg portion until the ball of the thighbone pops from the hip socket. Cut between the ball and socket and the leg portion will come away. Repeat to remove the other leg.

To divide the drumstick from the thigh, place each whole leg portion on a cutting board, skin side down. Cut firmly through the joint between the drumstick and thigh to separate them into two pieces. If the bird is very small, you can omit this step and treat the leg portion as one piece.

Next, remove the wings by pressing the top bone (the one connected to the body) of one wing against the bird's body, so you can feel the shoulder ball-and-socket joint. Make an incision between the ball and socket, then pull the wing away from the body and cut down through the skin at the base of the wing. A thin slice of the breast meat will come away with the wing. Repeat to remove the other wing. (If desired, you can separate the top bone from the wing in the same manner that you separated the thigh and drumstick. These two pieces are often what you receive when you order Buffalo chicken wings.)

With the bird still breast side up, halve the carcass by starting on one side of the bird and making a cut that runs parallel to the backbone and slicing through the bones of the rib cage from the tail end through the thin area until you get to the shoulder joint. Repeat the same process on the opposite side of the bird's backbone.

Remove the breast by pulling apart the breast and the back to expose the meat-covered shoulder blades that join them. Cut down through these bones to detach the breast section. Next, divide the back into two pieces by cutting across the backbone at the point where the rib cage of the chicken ends.

Then halve the breasts. Place them, skin side up, on the cutting board and, using a strong steady pressure on the knife, cut down the length of the breastbone to separate the breast into two pieces.

HOW TO MAKE CHICKEN CUTLETS

You can trim your budget a bit by cutting your own cutlets—generally the most expensive piece of chicken since you are paying for the butcher's cutting skills.

Here's how to do it yourself:

Place a boneless, skinless breast on a cutting board. Holding it flat with the palm of your hand and with a knife in the other hand, slice it in half horizontally so that you are cutting parallel with the cutting board. You've just butterflied the breast. Place the two halves on a cutting board and trim any ragged edges. Use the heel of your hand and press down to flatten each piece to a thickness of about ½ inch. You've just saved yourself $2 a pound by making chicken cutlets yourself.

HOW TO SKIN CHICKEN PARTS

Removing the skin removes much of the fat from a chicken, which can provide healthier dishes.

To skin a chicken thigh, grasp a corner of the skin firmly and pull it away in one piece.

To skin a chicken breast, grasp the skin at the thick end of the breast and pull it away.

To remove the skin from a drumstick, pull the skin from the meaty part down toward the end of the drumstick with a paper towel and pull off the entire skin.

WHAT IS BUTTERFLYING?

To butterfly a chicken means to cut it so that it lies flat like an open book. This method allows the chicken to cook quicker and exposes the skin to a larger surface of the pan. To butterfly a whole chicken, use poultry shears to cut down both sides of the backbone and remove it. I like to drop the backbones into a large freezer bag—adding additional backbones to the bag whenever cooking—until I have enough to make a big pot of stock. Place the chicken on a cutting board and, using the heels of your palm, press hard on the breastbone to break it and flatten the chicken.

WHAT IS A PAILLARD?

Pronounced *pahy-yard*, it is a French cooking technique that uses thinly sliced or pounded meat that is cooked quickly. To form a chicken paillard, place a chicken breast between two pieces of plastic wrap on a cutting board and use the flat side of a meat mallet to pound it carefully to the desired thickness. This a great way to cook chicken breasts when you are short on time, since the thinner cuts cook up very quickly—depending on the size of the pieces and how you cook them, it can be as quick as a minute on each side.

WHY DREDGE CHICKEN IN FLOUR?

The word *dredge* means to coat a food lightly in flour. Chicken or other thin cuts of meats that are to be fried are often first dredged in flour, then in beaten egg, and then in bread crumbs. But chicken parts are also often dredged in just flour. This allows everything to adhere well to the meat and not fall apart during cooking, and creates a crust that is golden and delicious.

To dredge, spread some flour in a shallow dish such as a glass pie plate. Pat the piece of chicken dry with a paper towel and season with salt and pepper. It works best if you season the chicken in addition to the flour to assure the actual flavor winds up on the meat and not in the leftover flour. Next dip the chicken in the flour and turn it over to coat. Take the piece out of the flour and shake it lightly over the dish to remove any excess flour. It's important to dredge foods just before cooking so that the coating doesn't absorb moisture from the chicken and get soggy.

AVOIDING TOUGH CHICKEN

One of the best ways to prevent your chicken from being tough is to be sure to cut your pieces against the grain. Poultry has bundles of muscle fibers that run the length of the breast, so cutting against the grain shortens the muscle fibers. Take a close look at a chicken breast—you will see there are distinct lines running through the meat. These long lines are fibers and can be difficult to chew through. If you slice the meat in the same direction as the fibers, you will have to chew through the fibers. But if you cut across the lines, the knife will have already done the work for you. Think of it like a slicing a stalk of celery. The strings are less likely to get caught in your teeth if you cut across the grains and not lengthwise with the strings. This works particularly well when cutting breast meat into strips or nuggets.

When slicing, it often helps to cut the meat on the diagonal, which makes for a nicer presentation.

TEMPERATURES

While the USDA recommends that a whole chicken be cooked to an internal temperature of 180°F—mostly to assure that all the bacteria have been killed—I find that temperature too high, often resulting in an overcooked and dry bird.

You should own an instant-read thermometer when working with chicken. I generally check the temperature of a whole chicken while it is still in the oven by inserting the tip of the thermometer into the thickest part of the thigh—toward the interior rather than exterior part of the bird—and removing the bird from the oven once the temperature registers 160°F. Make sure you do not touch the bone with the tip of the thermometer, or you will get a higher reading. It is best to allow the bird to rest at room temperature for about 20 minutes before carving. The bird will continue to cook from its own internal heat.

The temperatures below for grilling are for the method of indirect cooking where the heat source is located to the side of the chicken and not directly underneath where it will likely overcook the meat on the outside and undercook inside.

APPROXIMATE COOKING TIMES FOR WHOLE BIRDS

CHICKEN	WEIGHT	AT 350°F	GRILLING/INDIRECT METHOD
Whole Broiler-Fryer	3–5 pounds	1¼–1½ hours	1–1½ hours
Whole Roaster	5–7 pounds	2–2¼ hours	18–20 minutes per pound
Whole Capon	4–8 pounds	2–3 hours	15 minutes per pound
Cornish Hens	18–24 ounces	50–60 minutes	45–55 minutes

APPROXIMATE COOKING TIMES FOR PARTS

CHICKEN	WEIGHT	AT 350°F	GRILLING/INDIRECT METHOD
Boneless Breast	4 ounces	20–30 minutes	10 minutes per side
Legs or Thighs	4–8 ounces	40–50 minutes	10–15 minutes per side
Wings	2–3 ounces	30 minutes	8–12 minutes per side

GRILLING TEMPERATURES

High Heat	500–600°F
Medium-High Heat	450–500°F
Medium Heat	350–450°F
Low Heat	300–350°F

CARVING AND MAKING A SIMPLE PAN SAUCE

Before carving a chicken, let it rest at room temperature for at least 10 minutes and up to 20 minutes to allow the natural juices to redistribute. It will not get cold and will, in fact, continue to cook a bit.

The first step in carving the chicken is to remove the leg. Set the chicken, breast side up, on a cutting board and cut through the skin between the thigh and breast. Pull the leg away from the body to find the thigh joint. Then cut through the joint and remove the entire leg. If the chicken is small, serve the whole leg as a single portion. If it is large, cut through the joint that separates the drumstick from the thigh. To carve the thigh, cut off the meat in thin slices parallel to the bone. Be sure when you separate the leg that you get the "oyster," an especially tasty piece of chicken just above where the thigh connects to the body.

Remove the wing by cutting through the skin between the wing and breast and pulling the wing away from the body to locate the shoulder joint. Cut through the joint and remove the wing.

To carve the breasts, begin separating one side of the breast from the body by cutting along the breastbone with the tip of your knife. Your goal is to completely remove the breast from the rest of the chicken. When you reach the wishbone, angle the knife and cut down along the wishbone. Then cut down to the wing joint. Separate the breast from the carcass by pulling back on the meat and then with quick, short strokes, cut off the entire breast. Slice the breast crosswise, in half or into thin slices.

When carving, be sure to reserve the juices as they will make a great base for a nice sauce. When sautéing or braising, after the chicken has cooked, remove the chicken pieces from the pan and make a quick pan sauce. Add a bit of flour to any juices or fat that may be left in the pan. Add some liquid—water, chicken broth, or wine—and deglaze the pan by scraping up any brown bits remaining in the bottom of the pan. Whisk over medium heat until thickened. Serve the sauce as is or add other herbs or flavorings.

CHICKEN BROTH VERSUS CHICKEN STOCK: WHAT'S THE DIFFERENCE?

Chicken stock generally tends to be made from the chicken bones, while chicken broth is made from the meat of the chicken. Chicken stock has a richer, deeper chicken flavor due to the gelatin released from long-simmered bones. Chicken stock is especially good for things like chicken noodle soup when you want a richer chicken flavor.

A quick way to make a stock is to remove all the meat from a supermarket rotisserie chicken and toss the remaining carcass and bones into a pot of water with some vegetable scraps, salt and pepper, and some dried thyme. Let it cook for an hour or so and then strain.

Canned low-sodium chicken broth is a busy cook's best friend. As I've said before, salt is a big part of the cooking process, but I prefer to add it myself rather than have it added in the packaging process. So the low-sodium variety is what I choose. You can easily enhance the flavor of canned stock by adding some vegetables or vegetable scraps and simmering for as long as you can.

MAKING YOUR OWN CHICKEN STOCK

In my first book, *Mr. Sunday's Soups*, I offered an easy homemade chicken stock recipe. I repeat it here for you to use for a variety of recipes in this book. It's especially easy to make after you have cut up several chickens into 8 parts and removed the backbones. You can toss the backbones into a freezer bag and keep in the freezer until you have enough to make a big pot of stock.

Chicken Stock

6 pounds chicken bones (backbones, wings but no fat)

2 large yellow onions, peeled and quartered

4 large carrots, washed and roughly chopped

6 celery stalks, roughly chopped

6 sprigs fresh thyme

1 bay leaf

7 quarts water

In a large stockpot, combine the chicken bones, onions, carrots, celery, thyme, and bay leaf. Add the water and place over high heat. Bring to a boil, then adjust the heat so the liquid simmers gently, and cook, uncovered, for an hour. As soon as the chicken begins to release fat into the liquid, after about 10 minutes, begin degreasing with a large flat spoon; degrease every 10 or 15 minutes. Skim the surface of any visible fat; don't worry if you can't remove every bit.

Strain the stock through a fine-mesh sieve into a large, clean saucepan. Place over medium-high heat and simmer briskly until it has reduced by half, to about 3½ quarts; this will take about 20 minutes. Continue degreasing the stock as it reduces, if necessary. Use the stock immediately as directed in a recipe, or cool down quickly in an ice bath to room temperature and refrigerate in 2- or 4-cup quantities for up to a 1 week. The stock can also be frozen for up to 4 months.

Fall

After the dog days of hazy hot Washington, fall is a season that brings cooler weather, brilliant leaves, and Redskins football. The farmers' markets and vegetable gardens are bursting with beautiful ripe produce ready for picking!

This is the season I really get excited about being creative in the kitchen. Weekends mean visiting apple orchards and pumpkin patches, which is especially fun during the Indian summer of late September, when the days are warm, and the evenings are cool and crisp. My Honey-Mustard Chicken with Apples is a delicious recipe, which takes little time to make, so you can enjoy the beautiful outdoors with your friends and family and still enjoy a dish that is loaded with sweet apples, savory onions, and mustard.

And since everyone's schedule is in full swing and hectic, I created a simple Rotisserie Chicken à la King. Here in Washington, I think

opposite: Billy Martin and Lorraine in the kitchen at Martin's Tavern. *right:* Karen and Chris Cheda

Leonard family reunion: Thanksgiving 2010. Photo by Michael Bennett Kress.

Wagshal's market has the best rotisserie chicken in town. They use only hormone-free chickens, and their secret for preparing these tender, juicy chickens is using the chicken drippings to baste their birds. Call ahead on the weekends and reserve your chicken because they often run out of this local favorite.

Once again it is turkey time! My daughter Sarah loves when I take leftovers from our Thanksgiving meal and prepare Turkey Tetrazzini. This classic dish is just brimming with mushrooms that I load in the center of the casserole and top with Parmesan cheese for a golden, bubbly one-dish meal. All you need to complete this supper is a beautiful spinach salad with toasted pecans, sliced pears, and crumbled gorgonzola cheese.

All the poultry recipes I share with you for this glorious season have helped to make our family feel safe, nourished, and loved.

Wagshal's famous chicken. Photo by Brian Fuchs.

Rotisserie Chicken à la King

ROTISSERIE • QUICK • SERVES 6

This was a favorite dish that my mother made when I was growing up. Here I have re-created this classic by using a rotisserie chicken that saves time and makes it more modern. Chicken à la King can be presented either as a simple family meal just spooned over toast points, or served in puff pastry shells for a more elegant meal.

6 frozen store-bought puff pastry shells

1 tablespoon extra-virgin olive oil

1 cup diced onion

½ green bell pepper, seeded and diced

½ cup diced roasted red bell peppers

8 ounces button mushrooms, sliced

Coarse salt and freshly ground black pepper

½ cup (1 stick) unsalted butter

¼ cup all-purpose flour

2 cups chicken broth, homemade or store-bought

½ cup sherry wine

2 large egg yolks

½ cup heavy cream

1 rotisserie chicken, meat pulled and shredded or cubed (about 6 cups)

Preheat the oven to 425°F.

Bake off the frozen puff pastry shells according to the package directions (about 20 minutes). Keep them warm in a 200°F oven until ready to serve.

Meanwhile, in a large skillet over medium-low heat, warm the oil. Add the onion, green bell pepper, roasted red bell pepper, and mushrooms and cook, stirring, until the mushrooms have released all their liquid and the onions have begun to brown, about 5 minutes. Season with salt and pepper.

Add the butter and allow to melt. Add the flour and whisk together, until smooth. Gradually add the chicken broth, whisking to avoid lumps, and cook until the mixture begins to thicken. Add the sherry wine, egg yolks, and cream and stir until well combined. Fold in the chicken and cook until heated through, about 5 minutes. Taste and adjust the seasoning with salt and pepper, if needed.

Remove the tops from the pastry shells. Place each shell on a serving plate, and fill with the chicken à la king mixture. Serve immediately.

Martin's Chicken Marsala

From the kitchen of Chef Billy Martin

BONELESS, SKINLESS • STOVETOP • FAMILY FAVORITE • SERVES 4

Martin's Tavern is a Washington landmark that has been the home away from home to celebrities, movers and shakers, Hollywood stars, Broadway legends, and Georgetowners since 1933. The legendary restaurant and tavern has had the honor of serving every president from Harry Truman to George W. Bush. This is where JFK proposed to Jacqueline Bouvier and to this day, there is a booth at Martin's known as "The Proposal Booth."

Fourth-generation owner and manager, Billy Martin, invited me to lunch where he demonstrated how he prepares this delicious Chicken Marsala using their secret brown sauce. What a special treat!

4 boneless, skinless chicken breasts (about 8 ounces each)

1 cup all-purpose flour

Coarse salt and freshly ground black pepper

4 tablespoons extra-virgin olive oil

1 pound button mushrooms, sliced

1 cup Marsala wine

1 cup chicken broth, homemade or store-bought

4 tablespoons (½ stick) unsalted butter

Cooked Jasmine Rice (page 217), for serving

Rinse the chicken breasts with cold water and pat dry with paper towels. Place the flour in a shallow dish such as a glass pie plate and season with salt and pepper. Dredge the chicken breasts in the flour and shake off any excess.

Heat a sauté pan over medium-high heat and add 2 tablespoons of the oil. Add the mushrooms and cook, stirring, until browned, about 5 minutes. Transfer the mushrooms to a plate or bowl and set aside. To the same pan, add the remaining 2 tablespoons oil and brown the chicken breasts on each side, about 5 minutes per side. Transfer the chicken to a plate and set aside.

Deglaze the pan with the Marsala wine, scraping up any brown bits on the bottom of the pan. Add the chicken broth and simmer until reduced by half, about 5 minutes more.

Finish the sauce by adding the butter and stirring until it has melted and the sauce comes together. Return the chicken and mushrooms to the pan and stir to coat well with the sauce. Simmer for another 2 minutes.

Serve the chicken on warm dinner plates on top of a mound of jasmine rice.

Tandoori Roast Chicken

The Greek-style yogurt and ruby-colored spices make this chicken dish a wonderful bright golden orange color. Be sure to line your baking sheet with aluminum foil for a quick clean-up! I like to serve this family style on a large platter of basmati rice with the chicken piled on top and accompany it with my pickled cucumbers served in small individual glass bowls.

One 4-pound chicken, cut into 8 pieces, plus 1 pound chicken breasts, cut in half for a total of 12 pieces

1 cup Greek-style or plain yogurt

½ cup freshly squeezed lemon juice (about 2 lemons)

½ cup finely chopped white onion

6 garlic cloves, finely chopped

3 tablespoons peeled and grated fresh ginger

3 teaspoons paprika

2 teaspoons ground cumin

1 teaspoon cayenne pepper

¾ teaspoon ground turmeric

Nonstick cooking spray, for oiling the rack

2 tablespoons coarse salt

Rinse the chicken with cold water and pat dry with paper towels. Cut the chicken breasts in half crosswise. Put all the chicken in a large resealable plastic bag. In a large bowl, whisk together the yogurt, lemon juice, onion, garlic, ginger, paprika, cumin, cayenne, and turmeric. Transfer the marinade to the plastic bag and coat the chicken well by turning the bag over several times. Refrigerate for up to 8 hours or overnight.

Remove from the refrigerator up to 30 minutes prior to baking and keep turning the bag to coat the chicken.

Position a rack in the lower portion of the oven. Preheat the oven to 450°F. Line a baking sheet with aluminum foil, and coat a roasting rack with nonstick cooking spray. Place the rack on top of the lined baking sheet.

One by one, remove the chicken pieces from the bag, letting any excess marinade drip back into the bag, and place on the prepared roasting rack, skin side up, and in a single layer. Transfer the marinade to a bowl and reserve for basting.

Transfer the baking sheet to the oven and roast the chicken for 40 minutes, then brush with the reserved marinade. Move the baking sheet to the upper rack and continue to roast the chicken for 20 minutes more until golden. Discard the unused marinade. Remove the chicken from the oven and season with the salt to taste. Cover lightly with foil and let rest until ready to serve.

Chicken Marengo

BONELESS, SKINLESS • ONE POT • SERVES 4 TO 6

The classic French braised dish is traditionally made with veal. In the Wallace household, we enjoy this dish made with chicken. It is packed with mushrooms in a thick tomato-based sauce. The orange zest just adds a tasteful last note.

3 pounds boneless, skinless chicken breasts, cut into 2-inch pieces

¼ cup all-purpose flour

Coarse salt and freshly ground black pepper

7 tablespoons extra-virgin olive oil

1 large yellow onion, finely chopped (about 3 cups)

2 garlic cloves, minced

1½ cups dry white wine

1¼ cups canned crushed tomatoes, with their juices

½ teaspoon dried basil

½ teaspoon dried thyme

One ½-inch-wide strip orange zest, removed with a peeler

¾ pound egg noodles

1½ pounds button mushrooms, quartered

¼ cup finely chopped fresh flat-leaf parsley, for garnish

Position a rack in the middle portion of the oven, allowing enough space to hold a large Dutch oven. Preheat the oven to 325°F.

Rinse the chicken with cold water and pat dry with paper towels. Put the flour and salt and pepper in a large resealable plastic bag and shake to mix well. Place the chicken in the bag and shake until evenly coated with the seasoned flour.

In a large Dutch oven over medium-high heat, warm 3 tablespoons of the oil and swirl the pot to coat the bottom evenly. Add half of the chicken to the pot and cook until evenly browned on all sides, 4 to 6 minutes. Transfer the chicken to a large bowl or plate. Heat 2 more tablespoons of oil in the pot and cook the remaining half of the chicken. Transfer the chicken to the bowl or plate.

Add 1 tablespoon of the oil to the same pot. Add the onion and cook, stirring, until lightly browned and softened, about 5 minutes. Add the garlic and cook for 1 minute more. Add the wine and deglaze the pot, scraping up any brown bits on the bottom of the pot. Add the tomatoes and their juice, the basil, thyme, orange zest, and salt and pepper to taste and bring to a simmer.

Return the chicken to the pot and stir to combine well. Cover the pot, transfer it to the oven, and bake until the chicken is tender, about 1 hour.

Meanwhile, cook the egg noodles in a large pot of salted water according to the package directions. Drain well.

While the noodles are boiling, cook the mushrooms. In a skillet over medium-high heat, warm the remaining 1 tablespoon of oil. Add the mushrooms and cook, stirring, until they have softened and released their liquid, 6 to 8 minutes.

Remove the pot from the oven, uncover, and discard the zest. Add the mushrooms to the pot and stir to combine. Serve on warmed plates over the noodles, sprinkled with the parsley.

Chicken with Angel Hair Pasta and Rosemary Sauce

BONELESS, SKINLESS • QUICK • SERVES 4

This is a quick and simple one-dish meal that can be prepared in under 30 minutes. Not only is it delicious for dinner, but leftovers make a great lunch the next day.

8 ounces angel hair pasta

2 tablespoons extra-virgin olive oil

4 boneless, skinless chicken breast halves (about 6 ounces each)

¼ teaspoon coarse salt

¼ teaspoon freshly ground black pepper

½ cup chopped white onion

⅓ cup dry white wine

2 teaspoons minced fresh rosemary, plus extra for serving

½ cup chicken broth, homemade or store-bought

⅓ cup half-and-half

2 tablespoons chopped scallions, for garnish

In a large pot of boiling water, cook the pasta according to the package directions without any added salt or oil.

While the pasta is cooking, heat the oil in a large nonstick skillet over medium heat. Sprinkle the chicken with the salt and pepper, add to the pan, and cook until lightly browned, about 3 minutes per side. Add the onions, white wine, and rosemary and cook 30 seconds more. Stir in the broth and cook until the chicken is done, about 2 minutes. Add the half-and-half and cook for another 2 minutes.

Divide the pasta equally among four warm, wide-rimmed pasta bowls, place the chicken and sauce on top. Garnish with the scallions and chopped fresh rosemary.

Quick Chicken Stir-Fry

From the kitchen of Chantima

BONELESS, SKINLESS • QUICK • VEGGIE • SERVES 6

Chantima (aka Jim) is our housekeeper but really much more. She is a friend and we love to cook together. I have learned so much from her about her native country Thailand and their customs and cuisine. Here is Jim's stir-fry that our whole family loves to eat!

1½ pounds boneless, skinless chicken breasts

⅔ cup water

⅔ cup oyster sauce

1 tablespoon all-purpose flour

3 cups green beans (about 8 ounces), trimmed and cut in half crosswise

2 cups carrots (about 3 medium), peeled and cut into strips

2 tablespoons vegetable oil

1 small white onion, thinly sliced on the diagonal (about 2 cups)

1 small red bell pepper, seeded and thinly sliced on the diagonal (about 2 cups)

2 garlic cloves, minced

One 15-ounce can baby corn, drained and halved crosswise

Freshly ground black pepper

One 8.8-ounce package soba noodles

Soy sauce, for serving

Scallions, white and green parts, cut on a 2-inch diagonal, for garnish

Note: *For a vegetarian option, replace the chicken with cut-up tofu.*

Rinse the chicken with cold water and pat dry with paper towels. Cut the chicken into 1¼-inch pieces and place in a large bowl. Combine ⅓ cup of the water, ⅓ cup of the oyster sauce, and the flour in a small bowl and whisk to mix well. Pour over the chicken in the bowl and let marinate in the refrigerator for at least 1 hour.

Bring a pot of water to a boil. Add the green beans and blanch until bright green, about 2 minutes. Remove from the heat, transfer to a colander, and rinse under cold running water to stop the cooking. Repeat the procedure to blanch the carrots. Set aside.

Heat the oil over medium high heat in a wok or a skillet large enough to hold all of the ingredients. Add the onion and red bell peppers and stir-fry for 3 minutes. Add the garlic and stir-fry an additional 1 minute.

Add the chicken and the remaining ⅓ cup oyster sauce, toss to coat all the ingredients with the sauce, and cook, stirring, for 5 minutes. If the chicken is too dry, add the remaining ⅓ cup water to loosen the mixture. Stir in the reserved green beans, carrots, and the baby corn and cook for 1 minute to reheat the vegetables. Season to taste with black pepper.

Meanwhile, cook the soba noodles according to the package directions. Divide the noodles equally among six serving plates and top with the stir-fry. Garnish with the scallions and serve with a small bowl of soy sauce on the table.

Classic Chicken Pot Pie

If you are pressed for time or just have half of a chicken left, use a store-bought crust and roll it to top this classic dish or finish up with leftover roasted chicken to make this delicious pie.

FOR THE CRUST

2 cups all-purpose flour

¼ teaspoon coarse salt

12 tablespoons (1½ sticks) cold unsalted butter, cut into 10 pieces

1 large egg yolk, beaten, for brushing

FOR THE FILLING

2½ pounds boneless, skinless chicken thighs, or 5 cups rotisserie chicken meat, pulled and shredded or cubed

Coarse salt and freshly ground black pepper

5 tablespoons extra-virgin olive oil

8 ounces button mushrooms

1 cup frozen petite peas, defrosted

½ cup frozen pearl onions, defrosted

4 medium carrots, peeled and sliced crosswise into ½-inch-thick rounds

4 tablespoons (½ stick) unsalted butter

½ cup all-purpose flour

1 quart chicken broth, homemade or store-bought

½ cup dry white wine

1 cup half-and-half

To prepare the crust: Put the flour and salt in a food processor and pulse to blend. Add the butter and pulse until the butter pieces are the size of peas, 10 to 12 pulses. Drizzle 3 tablespoons of ice cold water over the mixture and pulse until the dough forms moist crumbs that are just beginning to clump together, about 9 pulses more. Turn the crumbs out onto a large piece of plastic wrap and gather into a pile. With the heel of your hand gently smear the dough away from you until the crumbs come together. Shape the dough into a square, wrap tightly in plastic wrap, and refrigerate until firm, for at least 2 hours or up to 2 days.

Position a rack in the middle portion of the oven. Preheat the oven to 350°F.

To prepare the filling: Rinse the chicken thighs with cold water and pat dry with paper towels. Season generously with salt and pepper. In a large Dutch oven over medium-high heat warm 2 tablespoons of the oil until very hot. Working in batches, brown the first chicken thighs, 4 to 5 minutes per side. Add 1 more tablespoon of the oil to cook the second batch. Transfer the chicken to a cutting board and cut into 1-inch pieces. (It is fine if the chicken is not cooked through, it will continue to cook in the pie.) Put the chicken in a large bowl and set aside.

Add 1 tablespoon of the oil to the pot, add the mushrooms and cook, without stirring, for 1 minute. Continue cooking, stirring occasionally, until browned, about 4 minutes. If the mushrooms are sticking to the pot, add a little of the broth. Transfer the mushrooms to the bowl of chicken and set aside.

(recipe continues on page 44)

(continued from page 42)

1 tablespoon Dijon mustard

¼ cup chopped fresh flat-leaf parsley

Nonstick cooking spray

Reduce the heat to medium and add the remaining 1 tablespoon oil. Add the peas, onions, and carrots and cook, stirring occasionally, until the edges are brown, 8 to 9 minutes. Transfer the vegetables to the bowl of chicken and mushrooms.

In the same pot over low heat, melt the butter. Add the flour and cook, whisking constantly, until the mixture is bubbling, 2 to 3 minutes. Gradually whisk in the chicken broth, wine, and half-and-half, scraping up any brown bits from the bottom of the pan, until the sauce is smooth. Bring to a slight boil, reduce the heat to low, and return the chicken and vegetables to the pot. Season with salt and pepper to taste and add the mustard and parsley. Partially cover the pot and simmer gently for 10 minutes, stirring occasionally. Taste and adjust the seasoning, if necessary.

Spray a 9-inch deep-dish pie plate with nonstick cooking spray. Pour the filling into the plate and set aside.

On a lightly floured surface, roll out the dough into a round large enough to cover the pie plate. Place the crust over the filling and make a few slits in the top so that the steam can escape. Trim off any overhanging dough with a knife. Using your fingers, crimp the edges and place the pie plate on a baking sheet, brush the crust with the beaten egg yolk, and bake for 30 minutes until golden.

Sausage Pasta Rustica

$ • ONE POT • SERVES 8

The hearty chicken or turkey sausage and three cheeses, combined with a lightly beaten egg, make this rustic dish rise up in the oven to a large one-dish golden casserole, perfect for a crisp fall supper. I like to serve it with an Italian-style salad.

2 tablespoons extra-virgin olive oil

1 large yellow onion, chopped

2 garlic cloves, minced

1½ pounds bulk sweet or mild turkey or chicken sausage, or 6 mild turkey sausages, meat removed from the casings

¼ teaspoon freshly ground black pepper

1 teaspoon dried basil

1 teaspoon dried oregano

¼ teaspoon crushed red pepper flakes

One 28-ounce can tomato puree

1 cup water

Nonstick cooking spray

Coarse salt

1 pound of penne or other tube-shaped pasta

1 large egg

2 cups ricotta cheese

2 cups shredded mozzarella cheese

½ cup freshly grated Parmesan cheese

In a large saucepan over medium-high heat, warm the oil. Add the onion and cook, stirring, until softened, about 5 minutes. Add the garlic and cook, stirring for 1 minute more. Add the sausage meat and brown, breaking it up into bite-size pieces with the side of a spoon, until the sausage is no longer pink, about 8 minutes. Stir in the pepper, basil, oregano, and red pepper flakes and cook for 2 minutes more.

Add the tomato puree and water and bring to a boil. Reduce the heat to low and simmer, uncovered, for about 20 minutes. Remove from the heat and cool slightly.

Preheat the oven to 350°F. Lightly spray a 13 × 9-inch shallow baking dish with nonstick cooking spray and set aside.

Bring a large pot three-fourths full of water generously sprinkled with salt to a boil. Add the pasta, stir well, and cook until barely al dente, about 12 minutes. Rinse with cold water and drain.

In a large bowl, lightly beat the egg with a whisk. Add the ricotta and mozzarella cheeses and mix well to combine. Add the drained pasta to the cheese mixture and mix to coat evenly, then add the sausage sauce and mix to combine all of the ingredients.

Pour the mixture into the prepared baking dish and sprinkle with the Parmesan cheese. Bake until the cheeses have melted and the tips of the pasta are crusty. Remove from the oven and let cool for about 5 minutes before serving.

Turkey Meatballs with Spaghetti Squash

ONE POT • SERVES 6

Squash is abundant in the fall, and that is when I like to prepare this lighter dish using spaghetti squash instead of pasta for a crisp fall night. With the addition of the spinach and luscious mushrooms, you really don't need to prepare anything else. This dish is a nutritious dinner on its own.

Nonstick cooking spray

1 spaghetti squash (about 4 pounds), halved lengthwise

Coarse salt and freshly ground black pepper

1 pound ground turkey

1½ cups plain dried bread crumbs

½ cup freshly grated Parmesan cheese, plus more to taste, for serving

3 large eggs, beaten

2 teaspoons dried Italian seasoning

½ teaspoon garlic powder

2½ tablespoons extra-virgin olive oil

1 small yellow onion, chopped (about 1 cup)

8 ounces fresh mixed mushrooms, such as shiitake, cremini, and oyster, cut into ¼-inch pieces

2 garlic cloves, minced

1 cup chicken broth, homemade or store-bought

6 cups fresh baby spinach, tough stems removed

(recipe continues on page 48)

Preheat the oven to 375°F. Line a baking sheet with aluminum foil and coat lightly with nonstick cooking spray.

Season the cut sides of squash with ¼ teaspoon salt and a sprinkle of pepper. Prick the flesh with a fork to allow steam to escape. Bake, cut sides down, on the prepared baking sheet for 1 hour, until tender. Set aside until cool enough to handle. Remove the seeds and discard, then, using a fork, scrape the flesh into strands. Cover and keep warm.

Meanwhile, make the meatballs by combining the ground turkey, bread crumbs, cheese, beaten eggs, Italian seasoning, and garlic powder in a large mixing bowl. Season with salt and pepper and mix well with your hands. Form the mixture into 1-inch balls.

Heat 1½ tablespoons of the oil in a large skillet over medium heat. Cook the meatballs, turning occasionally, to brown all sides, for 4 to 6 minutes. Using a slotted spoon, transfer the meatballs to a plate.

Add the remaining 1 tablespoon oil to the skillet, add the onion, and cook over medium-high heat, stirring occasionally, for about 3 minutes. Add the mushrooms and cook, stirring occasionally, until they begin to brown, about 5 minutes. Add the garlic and cook until fragrant, about 30 seconds. Add the broth, a pinch of salt and pepper, and the meatballs and bring to a gentle simmer. Cook, partially covered, until the meatballs are

(continued from page 47)

cooked through, about 5 minutes. Add the spinach and cook until just wilted, about 1 minute.

Serve the squash in a large pasta bowl, and ladle the meatball-vegetable mixture on top. Sprinkle with Parmesan cheese to taste.

Honey-Mustard Chicken with Apples

$ • QUICK • STOVETOP • SERVES 6

By combining the season's apples and sweet honey mustard, I can prepare this sweet and savory dish in just 30 minutes for a comforting but simple supper. While the chicken is finishing in the oven, I like to roast Sarah's Sweet Potato Wedges (page 227) to serve with this dish.

8 boneless, skinless chicken thighs (2 to 2½ pounds)

Coarse salt and freshly ground black pepper

2 tablespoons extra-virgin olive oil

1 large yellow onion, cut into large wedges

2 apples, cored, peeled, and cut into wedges

1 large fennel bulb, sliced (about 4 cups)

⅓ cup white wine

1 cup chicken broth, homemade or store-bought

3 tablespoons honey mustard

Hot cooked rice (optional), for serving

2 tablespoons chopped fennel fronds

Preheat the oven to 350°F.

Rinse the chicken with cold water and pat dry with paper towels. Season with salt and pepper. Heat the oil in a large ovenproof skillet over medium-high heat. Add the chicken and cook until golden on the bottom, about 6 minutes. Flip and cook the opposite sides, 2 to 3 minutes more. Transfer the chicken to a plate and pour off all but 2 tablespoons of the drippings from the skillet.

Add the onion, apples, and fennel to the skillet and season with salt and pepper. Cook, stirring occasionally, until slightly softened, about 5 minutes. Add the wine, deglaze the pan, and allow to cook for about 2 minutes. In a small bowl, mix the broth with the mustard, then add to the skillet and bring to a boil.

Return the chicken to the skillet, and transfer it to the oven, and roast until the chicken is cooked through, about 20 minutes. Serve the chicken and fruit over rice, if you like, and garnish with the fennel fronds.

Chicken Scaloppine with Pears

BONELESS, SKINLESS • QUICK • SERVES 4

Pears begin to come to farmers' markets and grocery stores in late fall. This is when I like to prepare this simple chicken dish, using this wonderful seasonal fruit.

3 tablespoons extra-virgin olive oil

½ cup cornstarch

1½ pounds boneless, skinless chicken breast halves, either thin-cut or pounded into cutlets

Coarse salt and freshly ground black pepper

¾ cup white grape juice

¾ cup chicken broth, homemade or store-bought

2 medium pears, cored and cut into ¼-inch-thick slices

1 small yellow onion, thinly sliced into half-moons

1 tablespoon unsalted butter

In a large skillet over medium-high heat, warm the oil. Spread the cornstarch out in a shallow dish or pie plate. Sprinkle the chicken cutlets with salt and pepper, then coat both sides with the cornstarch, shaking off any excess.

Cook the chicken in the skillet (in batches if necessary) being careful not to overcrowd the pan, until lightly browned on one side, about 4 minutes. Turn the pieces over and cook on the opposite sides for 3 minutes more. Transfer the chicken to a plate and cover loosely with aluminum foil.

Combine the white grape juice and broth in a measuring cup. Add the sliced pears and onion and about ⅓ cup of the juice-broth mixture to the skillet. Cook, stirring and scraping up the browned bits, for about 2 minutes. Allow some of the liquid to evaporate, then add the butter and stir to combine.

Reduce the heat to medium, and continue to cook until the pears and onions are tender, about 5 minutes. Add the remaining juice-broth mixture to the skillet and add the chicken, making sure all the chicken is coated with some of the cooking liquid and the pears and onions. Increase the heat to medium-high until the liquid comes to a boil. Then reduce to a simmer.

Cook for 5 minutes more, or until the sauce is thickened slightly and the chicken is cooked through. Serve the chicken on a platter with the pear-onion mixture spooned on top.

Thin-Cut Chicken Parmesan

BONELESS, SKINLESS • FAMILY FAVORITE • SERVES 6

When our children were in middle school, I decided to re-create this classic dish because whenever we would go out to steak houses to eat large steaks and lobsters, they would always order Chicken Parmesan. I make this one-dish meal for six portions because we are such a large family. But if you want to make it smaller, just cut the recipe in half to serve three.

1½ pounds chicken cutlets, ¼ inch thick (6 cutlets)

2 cups plain dried bread crumbs

1 cup finely grated Pecorino Romano or Parmesan cheese

½ teaspoon coarse salt

Pinch of freshly ground black pepper

¾ cup all-purpose flour

3 large eggs, beaten

¾ cup vegetable oil

2 cups marinara sauce

1 cup grated mozzarella cheese

Preheat the oven to 375°F.

Rinse the chicken cutlets with cold water and pat dry with paper towels. Place on a large plate. Combine the bread crumbs, Pecorino Romano, salt, and a grind of pepper in a shallow dish such as a pie plate. Put the flour and eggs in 2 separate shallow dishes. Dredge each cutlet in the flour, shaking off the excess. Dip in the eggs, letting any excess drip off. Then dredge in the bread-crumb mixture to coat. Place them on a baking sheet for 10 minutes.

Heat the oil in a large skillet over medium heat; the oil is ready when a bit of the bread-crumb mixture sizzles when dropped in. Working in batches, fry the cutlets until golden on each side, about 3 minutes per side. Transfer to a paper towel–lined baking sheet.

Lightly spray a 13 × 9-inch baking dish, then spread 1 cup of the marinara sauce in the bottom. Arrange the cutlets in a single layer on top. Top with the remaining 1 cup sauce, making sure to cover each piece, then sprinkle with the mozzarella. Cover with aluminum foil and bake until bubbling, about 10 minutes. Uncover and bake until the cheese has melted and is golden and bubbling, 5 to 8 minutes more.

Remove from the oven and let stand for 5 minutes before serving.

Turkey or Chicken Tetrazzini

POTLUCK • FAMILY FAVORITE • SERVES 12

I know my daughter Sarah likes our traditional Thanksgiving dinner, but I think she prefers this dish that I prepare the day after our big meal to use up all the leftover turkey. I like to serve this in a large oval casserole dish. I combine the pasta and mushrooms and then create a well in the center and pour in the turkey and sauce.

6 tablespoons (¾ stick) plus 2 teaspoons unsalted butter, plus more for greasing the dish

1 pound elbow macaroni

8 cups diced button mushrooms (about 2 pounds)

¼ cup white wine

¾ cup all-purpose flour

1 quart whole milk, heated

3 large eggs, lightly beaten

5 cups cubed cooked turkey or chicken

2 teaspoons coarse salt

Freshly ground black pepper

⅔ cup freshly grated Parmesan cheese

Preheat the oven to 350°F, with the rack set in the middle portion of the oven. Grease a 13 × 9-inch casserole dish with butter and set aside.

In a large pot of boiling salted water, cook the macaroni according to the package directions. Drain and set aside.

Heat the 2 teaspoons of butter in a large pan over medium heat. Add the mushrooms and the wine and cook until the liquid has evaporated, about 7 minutes. Remove from the heat.

Heat the 6 tablespoons of butter in a saucepan over medium heat, add the flour, and cook, whisking, until the roux is golden and bubbling, about 2 minutes. Gradually stir in the hot milk and cook, stirring constantly, until the sauce is smooth and thickened, about 10 minutes. Remove the sauce from the heat and when partially cooled, stir in the beaten eggs. Divide the sauce between the macaroni and the cooked turkey or chicken.

Add the macaroni to the prepared casserole dish along with the mushrooms. Make a large well in the middle of the pasta and add the sauced turkey or chicken. Season with the salt and pepper on top and sprinkle with the Parmesan cheese to cover. Bake for 20 to 30 minutes, until the top is golden and the casserole is heated through.

Country Chicken-and-Mushroom Fricassee

I add a lot of celery leaves when garnishing this recipe because Chris likes them so much that he picks them off the top of this dish leaving everyone else without any. I like to serve my Baked Brussels Sprouts (page 207) along with this mushroom-loaded dish.

3½ pounds chicken bone-in breasts, thighs, and wings

Coarse salt and freshly ground black pepper

2 tablespoons extra-virgin olive oil

1 large leek, white and light-green parts only, well washed and chopped

1 pound button mushrooms, quartered

2 garlic cloves, finely chopped

2 bay leaves

1 teaspoon dried thyme

1 cup dry white wine

2 cups chicken broth, homemade or store-bought

⅓ cup sour cream

⅓ cup Greek-style yogurt

1 cup celery leaves

Preheat the oven to 425°F.

Rinse the chicken with cold water and pat dry with paper towels. Arrange the chicken pieces on a roasting rack placed on a baking sheet. Season generously with salt and pepper. Roast the chicken in the center of the oven until cooked through and the skin is crisp, about 45 minutes.

Meanwhile, in a large deep skillet, heat the olive oil over medium heat. Add the leek and cook, stirring, until just softened, about 6 minutes. Add the mushrooms, increase the heat to high, and cook, stirring occasionally, until lightly browned, about 5 minutes. Add the garlic, bay leaves, and thyme and cook until fragrant, about 1 minute. Add the wine and cook until evaporated, about 5 minutes, scraping up any brown bits from the bottom of the skillet. Add the chicken broth and simmer until the mixture has reduced by half, about 15 minutes. Remove the mixture from the heat and add the sour cream and yogurt. Discard the bay leaves.

Place the chicken, skin side up, on a large serving platter and spoon the sauce over and around the chicken. Garnish with the celery leaves and serve.

Wagshal's Famous Roasted Hormone-Free Chicken

From the kitchen of Executive Chef Ann Marie James

$ • QUICK • SERVES 4

The secret to Wagshal's tender, juicy, and flavorful chicken is the addition of chicken drippings. When you cook your next whole chicken, or roast chicken parts, collect the drippings. These drippings from any previously roasted chicken can be put into ½-cup containers, cooled, and then frozen for future use. Warm the chicken drippings before brushing them on your next chicken for roasting.

FOR THE NATURAL MARINADE

1 tablespoon coarse salt

1 tablespoon celery salt

1½ teaspoons onion salt

1 tablespoon freshly ground black pepper

1 cup cold water

FOR THE CHICKEN

One 3¼-pound hormone-free chicken

1 tablespoon natural marinade (above)

½ cup chicken drippings

1 tablespoon Chef Paul Prudhomme's Magic Seasoning Blends Meat Magic

Coarse salt and freshly ground black pepper

1 cup extra-virgin olive oil

1 tablespoon paprika

To prepare the marinade: In a bowl, combine the dry ingredients with the water and stir to dissolve.

To prepare the chicken: Rinse the chicken inside and out with cold water and pat dry with paper towels. Add the chicken and natural marinade mixture to a large bowl and let marinate for 2 to 3 hours in the refrigerator.

Preheat the oven to 350°F.

Remove the chicken from the bowl and place on a roasting rack in a roasting pan. Pour or brush ½ cup of collected (or reserved) chicken drippings over the chicken. Sprinkle with Meat Magic and salt and pepper. Place the chicken on the middle rack of the oven and roast for 30 minutes. Rotate the chicken and continue roasting for 30 minutes more. Insert an instant-read thermometer in the thickest part of the chicken leg, avoiding the bone; the chicken is done when the thermometer registers 165°F to 170°F.

In a small bowl, mix together the olive oil and paprika. Remove the chicken from the oven and brush with the paprika mixture. Save the drippings from the roasted chicken in ½-cup portions and store tightly covered in the freezer to use at a later date.

Chicken Enchiladas

BONELESS, SKINLESS • POTLUCK • FAMILY FAVORITE • SERVES 8

When my children were all still at home and in high school they loved our local restaurant, Cactus Cantina, so much that I decided to re-create this large one-dish meal to satisfy their cravings for Mexican food.

Nonstick cooking spray

2 tablespoons canola oil

1½ cups chopped onion

2 garlic cloves, minced

2½ cups chopped, cooked boneless, skinless chicken breasts

One 15-ounce can diced tomatoes, with the juice

One 4-ounce can diced green chilies, undrained

1 cup heavy cream

2 tablespoons all-purpose flour

One 11-ounce can green tomatillos, drained

1 cup chicken broth, homemade or store-bought

2 teaspoons ground cumin

2 teaspoons chili powder

½ teaspoon coarse salt

2 cups shredded Monterey Jack and cheddar cheese, mixed

Eight 6-inch flour tortillas

Preheat the oven to 350°F. Coat a 13 × 9-inch baking dish with nonstick cooking spray.

Heat the oil in a large nonstick skillet over medium-high heat. Add the onion and cook, stirring occasionally, until tender, about 5 minutes. Add the garlic and cook for 1 minute more. Stir in the chicken, tomatoes, and chilies. Reduce the heat and simmer until the liquid has evaporated by half, about 8 minutes. Remove from the heat and set aside to cool.

In a small saucepan over medium-high heat, combine the cream and flour and cook, whisking constantly, until the mixture thickens, about 5 minutes. Stir in the tomatillos, broth, ground cumin, chili powder, and salt. Bring to a boil, reduce the heat to a simmer, and cook until thickened, about 20 minutes. Set the mixture aside to cool, then puree in a blender until smooth.

Spoon ½ cup of the chicken mixture and 2½ tablespoons of the cheese down the center of each tortilla and roll up.

Arrange the filled tortillas in the bottom of the baking dish. Cover with the pureed tomatillo-cream mixture. Sprinkle with the remaining 1 cup of shredded cheese. Bake for 25 minutes, or until the cheese is bubbling and brown. Remove from the oven and let stand for 10 minutes before serving.

Skoda's Braised Chicken with Mushrooms and Cashews

From the kitchen of Chris Skoda

STOVETOP • SERVES 4

Chris was Remick's roommate at Rhodes College for two years. Over the years I have become good friends with him and his mom, Karen. We have spent hours cleaning and organizing their dorm room over the years. Now, we just make sure to schedule our trips to Memphis, so we can have fun together and not clean. We have given up on trying to sort these two guys out!

7 tablespoons extra-virgin olive oil

8 chicken thighs, bone-in, skin on

½ teaspoon coarse salt

8 ounces pancetta, cut into ½-inch pieces

2 large Spanish onions, sliced

Pinch of crushed red pepper flakes

5 garlic cloves, minced into a paste with ¼ teaspoon salt

2 pounds assorted mushrooms (cremini, shiitake, oyster) wiped clean with a towel and sliced

2 cups white wine

4 to 5 cups chicken broth, homemade or store-bought

1 tablespoon chopped fresh thyme

3 bay leaves

½ cup cashews, toasted until fragrant

4 garlic cloves, sliced

1 pound fresh spinach leaves

Coat a large, deep skillet with 2 tablespoons of the oil and place over high heat. Pat the chicken dry, season generously with salt, and place, skin side down, in the skillet. Cook until the skin is brown and crispy, reducing the heat, if necessary. Turn the chicken over to brown the other side. Remove the chicken from the pan.

Pour off the extra fat from the skillet and reduce the heat to medium-high. Add the pancetta and brown until crispy. Add the onions, season with salt and red pepper flakes, and sweat over medium heat, stirring occasionally, for 7 to 8 minutes. Add the garlic and continue cooking for 1 to 2 minutes. Add the mushrooms, season with salt, and continue cooking until they release their liquid. Add the wine and continue cooking until it has reduced by half. Return the chicken to the skillet and add the broth to cover. Add the thyme and bay leaves. Bring to a boil, reduce to a simmer, and continue cooking for 30 to 35 minutes.

Using a food processor fitted with the steel blade, process the toasted cashews, drizzled with 3 tablespoons of oil, to make a paste. Season with salt and set aside.

Coat a separate skillet with 1 tablespoon olive oil set over medium heat, add the garlic and cook, stirring, until golden, about 1 minute. Add the spinach leaves, toss with the remaining olive oil and garlic, and cook for about 2 minutes. Increase the heat and continue to cook until the spinach has wilted, about 1 minute more. Set aside.

Remove the chicken from the skillet. Taste the sauce and adjust the seasonings, if necessary. Stir in the cashew paste, bring to a boil, reduce to a simmer, and cook until thickened.

Using a slotted spoon, transfer the sautéed spinach to a serving platter and arrange the chicken on top. Pour the sauce over the chicken and serve.

Winter

Winter ushers in the cold as well as the snow school-age children hope for. It is also the holiday season when we decorate our houses, bake all kinds of treats, and prepare roasted dishes. I look forward to staying home and working on projects, with my kitchen smelling of a classic roasted chicken or a simple braise of coq au vin. It is also the time we gather with our friends and family for festive meals.

The longer cooking times for these winter favorites make for heartier dishes to serve your family that will help to keep them warm and healthy through this cold season. My housekeeper and friend, Chantima, roasts a classic herb chicken in which she cooks the chicken on a bed of vegetables for over an hour, after which she makes a light vegetable-based gravy that is lower in calories than traditional gravy and delicious served on top of her mashed potatoes. Chicken in a Pot is a dish that you bake in the oven and then serve right at the table. It is filled with carrots, onions, rosemary, and white turnips for a twist on the classic recipe.

The oven is not the only way to make comforting recipes to feed your family. You can also use your stovetop to prepare satisfying meals, like my Stovetop Chicken Cacciatore or Polenta Gratin with Turkey Bolognese, which take a little longer to make, but are scrumptious and warming to eat on a brisk day when there is a nip in the air.

Award-winning photographer and author of numerous books, friend, and cover photographer of this book, Nancy Ellison, shares with us her easy Braised Chicken in Orange Juice. Nancy's elegant recipe has a Mexican flare, but is easy to adapt using other ingredients to create variations with other ethnic flavors. When I make this recipe for my family, I have to chase them out of the kitchen because the house smells so good from all the spices in the skillet simmering on the stove.

When I have the whole family coming in for the holidays, I like to make recipes that will feed a larger group but are still festive. This is when I make Citrus-Chili Cornish Hens with Lemon Sauce and serve them with a casserole of Baked Brown Rice. Individual Chicken and Winter Vegetable Pot Pies are another favorite of mine to prepare. Instead of using the usual vegetables combined in the filling of these pies, I like to use different ingredients, such as celery root and parsnips, which are local ingredients at most markets during the winter. Another elegant supper I like to prepare is Holiday Lemon Chicken and Panko Green Beans with Slivered Almonds. You prepare

the chicken with orange blossom honey and bake the lemons whole in the dish along with the chicken, then serve straight from the oven to the buffet. Panko are Japanese bread crumbs that are coarser than regular dried bread crumbs and stick to the green beans. The almonds add the finishing touch to this dish for an elegant presentation.

One of our favorite neighborhood restaurants in Washington is Al Tiramisu, where chef and owner Luigi Diotaiuti prepares a classic Tuscan Duck Stew, which he shares with you in this chapter. Luigi likes to make this dish two ways: one as a *primi piatti* in which he shreds the duck after it is braised and serves it on top of pappardelle pasta. In his second version, he leaves the bone in the duck pieces and serves them on top of the sauce with braised fennel and polenta or herbed mashed potatoes. Be sure to ask for chef Luigi if you go to Al Tiramisu, and tell them Lorraine sent you!

top: Chantima and me. Photo by Nancy Ellison. *above:* Michael Psaltis and me. *right:* Bill Rollnick and his lovely wife Nancy Ellison. Photo by Leslie Bricusse. *opposite, top:* Winston waiting to open his stocking, 2010. *opposite, bottom:* Megan recently engaged, Christmas 2010

Polenta Gratin with Turkey Bolognese

This is a classic recipe with a twist since it uses polenta instead of the traditional pasta, and ground turkey instead of beef or pork. The tangy tomato Bolognese, made with ground turkey, is a recipe that Chantima learned to perfect while she was working with an Italian family. The sauce is especially good when it is made several days ahead.

FOR THE BOLOGNESE

2 tablespoons extra-virgin olive oil

1 large yellow onion, finely chopped (about 2 cups)

2 garlic cloves, finely minced

2½ pounds ground turkey

1 cup dry white wine

1 cup whole milk

2 tablespoons tomato paste

One 28-ounce can crushed tomatoes

One 15-ounce can tomato sauce

2 tablespoons dried oregano

2 bay leaves

1 teaspoon coarse salt

1 teaspoon freshly ground black pepper

FOR THE GRATIN

Unsalted butter, for greasing the pan

Two 18-ounce store-bought tubes prepared polenta

½ cup freshly grated Parmesan cheese

3 tablespoons fresh flat-leaf parsley or basil, minced

To make the Bolognese sauce: In a large heavy-duty saucepan, heat the oil over medium-high heat. Add the onion and cook, stirring, until soft and translucent, 4 to 5 minutes. Add the garlic and cook for 1 minute more. Add the ground turkey and brown, stirring to break it up, until it is no longer pink, about 10 minutes.

Add the white wine and let simmer until evaporated, about 15 minutes. Add the milk and continue to simmer for 15 minutes more. Add the tomato paste and cook until the raw flavor disappears, about 3 minutes. Add the crushed tomatoes and the tomato sauce and stir well to coat the meat. Season with the dried oregano, bay leaves, salt, and pepper. Bring to a boil, then reduce the heat to low and simmer for at least 1 hour. Remove and discard the bay leaves.

Preheat the oven to 400°F. Butter a 13 × 9-inch casserole dish.

To make the gratin: Remove the polenta from its plastic tube and cut each cylinder crosswise into slices about ¼ inch thick. Arrange the slices, overlapping them, in the prepared dish. Spoon the sauce around the polenta and sprinkle the Parmesan over the sauce. Bake until the sauce is hot and bubbly, about 20 minutes. Serve sprinkled with the parsley or basil.

Coq au Vin

Red wine, mushrooms, and pearl onions transform ordinary chicken into a French regional dish that can be made in any American kitchen right on the stovetop. This is especially flavorful when made a day ahead and reheated later for a great meal.

2 tablespoons unsalted butter

2 tablespoons diced onion

2 garlic cloves, minced

8 ounces button mushrooms, sliced

One 16-ounce bag frozen pearl onions

1 teaspoon coarse salt

1 teaspoon freshly ground black pepper

4 ounces bacon, sliced

3 whole chicken breasts, bone-in

3 chicken thighs, bone in, skin on

3 chicken drumsticks, bone in, skin on

One 700-milliliter bottle red wine

2 tablespoons all-purpose flour

1 tablespoon tomato paste

In a large Dutch oven over medium-high heat, melt the butter. Add the diced onions and garlic and cook, stirring, until the onions are translucent, 3 to 5 minutes. Add the mushrooms, pearl onions, salt, and pepper and continue to cook, stirring occasionally, until the onions begin to brown, about 5 minutes. Transfer the onions and mushrooms to a large bowl and set aside.

In the Dutch oven, fry the bacon until cooked. Transfer the bacon pieces to the bowl with the onions and mushrooms but reserve the bacon drippings in the pot. Add the chicken pieces to the pot and brown, turning once to brown the opposite sides, about 5 minutes per side. Add ¼ cup of the wine and deglaze the pot by scraping up all the browned bits on the bottom. Add the flour and cook, stirring, for about 1 minute to cook off the raw taste. Return the vegetables and bacon to the pot, cover with the remaining wine, and stir in the tomato paste. Bring to a simmer, cover the pot, and cook for 1 hour. Remove the lid and continue to simmer until the sauce thickens, about 15 minutes.

Half-Hour Chicken and Leek Stew

BONELESS, SKINLESS • QUICK • STOVETOP • SERVES 8

Using the stovetop to prepare this stew will make your home smell like a crisp day in the country! The aromatic chicken, vegetables, and thyme when combined with the Dijon mustard at the end of cooking makes your mouth water. Serve this with my French Lentils (page 201), Chris's favorite side dish.

2 pounds boneless, skinless chicken breasts

2 tablespoons butter

2 tablespoons extra-virgin olive oil

4 medium leeks, white and tender green parts only, well washed and thinly sliced

16 ounces cremini mushrooms, thinly sliced

Coarse salt and freshly ground black pepper

All-purpose flour, for dusting

3 cups chicken broth, homemade or store-bought

2 tablespoons chopped fresh thyme

¼ cup sour cream

4 teaspoons Dijon mustard

1 teaspoon fresh lemon zest

2 tablespoons fresh flat-leaf parsley, chopped

Warm, crusty bread, for serving

Rinse the chicken breast with cold water and pat dry with paper towels. Cut into 2-inch pieces.

In a Dutch oven over medium-high heat, warm the butter. Add the leeks and cook, stirring, until softened, about 8 minutes. Add the mushrooms, season with salt and pepper, cover, and cook, stirring, until the mushrooms are tender, about 4 minutes. Transfer the vegetable mixture to a plate and set aside.

Season both sides of the chicken pieces with salt and pepper and coat lightly with flour, shaking off any excess. Heat the oil in the Dutch oven, add the chicken, and cook over medium-high heat until golden brown, about 4 minutes per side. Add the chicken broth and thyme and simmer until the chicken is just cooked through, about 5 minutes.

Using a slotted spoon, transfer the chicken to the plate with the vegetables. Simmer the broth over medium-high heat until it has reduced by half, 3 to 4 minutes. Return the chicken and vegetables to the pot and simmer over low heat until warmed through, about 2 minutes.

In a small bowl blend the sour cream with the mustard and lemon zest and stir into the sauce. Remove the pot from the heat and stir in the parsley. Taste and adjust the seasoning with additional salt and pepper, if needed. Divide the stew equally among eight warm, wide-rimmed bowls and serve with warm crusty bread for dipping.

Chantima's Herb-Roasted Chicken with Vegetable Gravy

FAMILY FAVORITE • SERVES 6

This is Chantima's (aka Jim's) recipe for comforting roasted chicken in which she uses the vegetables and pan juices to prepare a light gravy. On cold days, we enjoy this chicken with Jim's creamy mashed potatoes. She boils the potatoes in their skins before peeling, which makes them extra soft for a quick mash.

One 4½- to 5-pound chicken

Coarse salt and freshly ground black pepper

1 tablespoon dried tarragon

6 tablespoons (¾ stick) unsalted butter, at room temperature

1 onion, diced

2 celery stalks, thinly sliced

2 medium carrots, peeled and thinly sliced

2 garlic cloves, mashed

1 cup dry white wine

2 cups chicken broth, homemade or store-bought

Rinse the chicken inside and out with cold water and pat dry with paper towels. Rub the chicken generously with salt and pepper and the tarragon.

Position a rack in the middle portion of the oven. Preheat the oven to 350°F.

In a skillet over medium-high heat, melt 1 tablespoon of the butter. Add the onion, celery, carrots, and garlic and cook, stirring, until just softened, about 5 minutes. Add the white wine and cook for 3 minutes more. Remove the skillet from the heat and add 1 cup of the chicken broth. Transfer the vegetable and broth mixture to a roasting pan. Place the chicken on top of the vegetables, breast side down, and brush with some of the remaining room-temperature butter to coat.

Roast for 1 hour, then turn the chicken breast side up and brush with more butter to coat. Cook for 30 minutes more, brushing with butter about every 15 minutes, until golden brown. Remove the roasting pan from the oven and transfer the chicken to a serving platter. Cover loosely with aluminum foil.

Transfer the vegetables from the roasting pan to a large pot and add the remaining 1 cup broth. Cook the vegetable-broth mixture until it has reduced to about 1¼ cups.

(continued on page 66)

(continued from page 65)

Place a strainer over a small saucepan and pour the vegetable-broth mixture into the strainer. Using a big spoon, mash the vegetables against the strainer into the broth mixture to make the gravy. Discard any remaining vegetable solids still in the strainer. Warm the gravy in the saucepan over low heat. Taste and adjust the seasoning with additional salt and pepper, if needed.

Crispy Pan-Roasted Chicken with Garlic-Thyme Butter

QUICK • STOVETOP • SERVES 4

This golden chicken dish is ready in under a half-hour and is especially delicious when served with my Gruyère Cheese au Gratin Potatoes (page 214). It is a perfect supper for a cold winter night.

One 3½-pound whole chicken,

1 tablespoon coarse salt

1 teaspoon freshly ground white pepper

2 tablespoons extra-virgin olive oil

2 tablespoons unsalted butter, at room temperature

1 teaspoon minced garlic

2 teaspoons finely chopped fresh thyme leaves

1 teaspoon finely chopped fresh rosemary

1 teaspoon finely chopped fresh oregano

Preheat the oven to 400°F.

Remove the breastbone, backbone, and wing tips of the chicken. Cut the remaining chicken into four pieces. Rinse the chicken with cold water and pat dry with paper towels. Season the chicken pieces on both sides with the salt and pepper.

Set a large, ovenproof cast-iron skillet over high heat and when it is hot, add the oil. Add the chicken pieces, skin side down, and sear until golden, about 3 minutes. Transfer the skillet to the oven and roast the chicken until it is nearly cooked through and the skin is crispy, 15 to 17 minutes. Turn the chicken over and continue to roast, skin side up, until it is cooked through, about 5 minutes more.

While the chicken is roasting, combine the butter with the garlic and spices in a small bowl and stir well to blend. As soon as the chicken is removed from the oven, spread the garlic butter over the skin and serve immediately.

Individual Winter Vegetable and Chicken Pot Pies

ROTISSERIE CHICKEN • SERVES 6

I like to bake the puff pastry for these pot pies separately from the filling because otherwise the crust gets too damp and soggy. Here the puff pastry is cut and baked on its own, which allows it to achieve its perfect golden flakiness. If you are not serving six people, you can defrost and bake only the number of pastry shells you need; the extra filling can be kept in the refrigerator in an airtight container for 3 days or frozen for up to 1 month.

FOR THE FILLING

1 rotisserie chicken, meat pulled and shredded

2½ tablespoons unsalted butter

4 cups total ½-inch-cubed mixed root vegetables, such as parsnips, carrots, butternut squash, sweet potatoes, or celery root

3 cups chicken broth, homemade or store-bought

1 cup frozen pearl onions, defrosted

2 strips thick-sliced bacon, cut crosswise into 1-inch pieces

2 garlic cloves, thinly sliced

1 tablespoon finely chopped fresh rosemary

2 tablespoons all-purpose flour

1 cup heavy cream

Coarse salt and freshly ground black pepper

Place the shredded chicken in a large bowl.

Position the racks in the lower portion of the oven. Preheat the oven to 400°F.

To make the filling: In a medium Dutch oven over medium-high heat, melt 1 tablespoon of the butter. Add the cubed vegetables and cook, stirring, just until softened, about 5 minutes. Add the broth and the onions, bring to a simmer, and cook, partially covered, for 7 minutes more. Strain the vegetables over a bowl, place them in another bowl, and reserve the broth.

In a medium nonstick skillet, cook the bacon over medium-high heat until lightly golden, about 5 minutes. Stir in the garlic and rosemary and cook for another minute until fragrant. Using a slotted spoon, transfer to the bowl with the vegetables and chicken.

Add the remaining 1½ tablespoons butter to the skillet and melt over medium-high heat, then stir in the flour. Reduce the heat to low and cook the roux, whisking constantly, for about 3 minutes until golden and bubbling.

Remove the skillet from the heat, add the heavy cream, and stir to combine. Stir the cream mixture into the chicken and vegetable mixture. Add ½ cup of the reserved broth and salt and pepper to taste and stir to combine well.

FOR THE CRUST

1 sheet frozen puff pastry, defrosted according to package instructions

1 large egg yolk, lightly beaten with a touch of cold water

Coarse salt and freshly ground black pepper

Transfer the mixture evenly to six eight-ounce ovenproof soup bowls. Cover with aluminum foil and keep warm.

To prepare the crust: Line a baking sheet with parchment paper. Unfold the puff pastry onto a clean, lightly floured surface. Cut into 6 rounds to fit the tops of the individual soup bowls. Place on the prepared baking sheet. Brush the tops with the egg wash. Sprinkle with salt and pepper. Bake in the oven according to the package directions. Place each round on top of the bowls filled with the warm chicken mixture and serve immediately.

Turkey Meat Loaf with Home-Style Gravy

GOOD FOR COMPANY • SERVES 6

By adding a little water to this turkey meat loaf when baking, you create not only a moist loaf but also a nice fat-free base to make the herb gravy. The gravy is delicious on both the sliced meat loaf and Classic Mashed Potatoes (page 204).

FOR THE MEAT LOAF

Nonstick cooking spray

1 large egg

2 tablespoons tomato paste

Coarse salt and freshly ground black pepper

½ cup chicken broth, homemade or store-bought

2 pounds ground turkey, either dark or breast meat

1 cup plain dried bread crumbs

1 medium yellow onion, finely chopped

2 celery stalks, finely chopped

3 tablespoons chopped fresh flat-leaf parsley

3 teaspoons chopped fresh rosemary or 1 teaspoon dried

¼ cup water

Classic Mashed Potatoes (page 204), (optional), for serving

FOR THE GRAVY

3 tablespoons unsalted butter

3 tablespoons all-purpose flour

Pan juices plus enough chicken broth, homemade or store-bought, to make 2 cups total

3 teaspoons chopped fresh sage or 1 teaspoon dried sage

Coarse salt and freshly ground black pepper

Preheat the oven to 350°F and lightly coat a 5 × 9-inch loaf pan with nonstick cooking spray.

To make the meat loaf: In a medium bowl, whisk together the egg, tomato paste, 1 teaspoon salt, and ½ teaspoon pepper until well combined. Add the chicken broth and stir to combine. Add the turkey, bread crumbs, onion, celery, parsley, and rosemary and mix until combined. Pack the mixture into the prepared loaf pan. Using a knife, make 6 small incisions in the meat loaf and pour a little water into each incision.

Bake the meat loaf in the center of the oven for about 1 hour and 15 minutes, or until an instant-read thermometer inserted in the center of the loaf registers 165°F. Transfer the loaf to a warmed platter and tent with aluminum foil to keep it warm. Reserve the liquid in the pan to make the gravy.

To make the gravy: In a small saucepan, melt the butter over low heat. Whisk in the flour and cook for 1 minute. Slowly whisk in the broth and reserved cooking liquid and stir to combine well. Increase the heat to medium and bring the gravy to a boil, then reduce the heat to medium-low and simmer until slightly thickened and reduced, about 5 minutes. Strain the gravy, add the sage, if using, and adjust the seasoning with additional salt and pepper, if needed. Pour the gravy into a warmed sauceboat. Serve the meat loaf on warm plates with mashed potatoes, if desired, and pass the gravy.

Stovetop Chicken Cacciatore

STOVETOP • SERVES 4

When I want to make a true Italian recipe, I get inspiration from re-reading Rao's, Recipes from the Neighborhood by Frank Pellegrino. This simple stovetop recipe is adapted from the book, and I hope you will enjoy it as much as our family does.

One 3- to 4-pound chicken, cut into 10 pieces

1 teaspoon coarse salt

1 teaspoon freshly ground black pepper

1 cup all-purpose flour

2 tablespoons extra-virgin olive oil

3 onions, sliced

1 carrot, peeled and diced

1 green bell pepper, seeded and cut into strips

3 garlic cloves, chopped

1 cup red wine

One 15-ounce can crushed tomatoes

1 cup sliced button mushrooms

3 tablespoons chopped fresh flat-leaf parsley

Rinse the chicken pieces with cold water and pat dry with paper towels. Season the pieces with the salt and pepper.

Put the flour in a shallow dish such as a pie plate. Dredge the chicken pieces in the flour and place on a rack or baking sheet.

Heat the oil in a skillet over medium-high heat. Add the chicken pieces and brown for about 5 minutes on each side; there is no need to cook the chicken pieces through, they will finish cooking in the sauce. Remove the chicken pieces from the skillet and place on a paper towel–lined plate.

Add the onions, carrot, green bell pepper, and garlic to the skillet and cook, stirring, until the onions are translucent, about 4 minutes. Reduce the heat to a simmer and add the wine to the vegetables. Scrape to remove all the bits of meat and vegetables attached to the bottom of the skillet. Increase the heat to medium-high and cook for 5 minutes more to allow some of the wine to reduce slightly.

Add the chicken pieces and tomatoes, making sure the chicken is covered with some of the vegetables and tomatoes. Cover the skillet, reduce the heat, and simmer slowly for 40 minutes.

Remove the cover, add the mushrooms, and simmer for 10 to 15 minutes more. Garnish with the parsley.

Balsamic Butterflied Chicken with Roasted Vegetables

$ • ONE POT • SERVES 4 TO 6

When this simple chicken emerges from the oven, it smells sweet from the onions and balsamic vinegar. I like to eat this at room temperature for a light lunch the next day since it is packed with vegetables. This is one of my favorite recipes because once it is prepared, I can walk away.

One 3- to 3½-pound chicken

Coarse salt and freshly ground black pepper

4 medium carrots, peeled and sliced into ½-inch-thick rounds

1 pound petite white whole potatoes or medium fingerlings, halved lengthwise

1 medium sweet onion, peeled and cut into 6 wedges

3 medium sprigs fresh thyme

2 medium sprigs fresh rosemary

3 tablespoons balsamic vinegar

3 tablespoons chicken broth, homemade or store-bought

2 tablespoons extra-virgin olive oil

Rinse the chicken inside and out with cold water and pat dry with paper towels. Butterfly the chicken by removing the backbone with kitchen scissors. (See What is Butterflying? on page 25.) Season the inside with salt and pepper and set aside.

Position a rack in the middle portion of the oven. Preheat the oven to 500°F.

Place the carrots, potatoes, and onion wedges in a 12-inch, cast-iron skillet. Tuck the herb sprigs among the vegetables. Place the chicken on top of the vegetables, breast side up, tucking the wing tips under.

Combine the balsamic vinegar, chicken broth, and oil in a small bowl and pour evenly over the top of the chicken. Place the skillet in the oven and roast the chicken and vegetables for 15 minutes.

Reduce the oven temperature to 400°F and continue to roast for 25 minutes more, or until a meat thermometer when inserted in the thickest part of the breast registers 165°F. Remove the skillet from the oven and let the chicken rest for 15 minutes, loosely covered with aluminum foil.

Carve the chicken into 6 pieces and serve with the vegetables and any of the pan juices on the side.

Turkey Burgers with Pimiento Spread

FAMILY FAVORITE • SERVES 4

Sometimes called the "pâté of the South," pimiento spread is little more than a combination of grated cheddar cheese, mayonnaise, and jarred chopped pimientos. Many Junior League cookbooks refer to it as the "Darling of the South," "Southern Charmer," and "Carolina Caviar." I've added a few drops of hot sauce and chopped pickles to my recipe. The spread is traditionally just served as a cocktail nibble smeared on crisp celery stalks but, as you are about to find out, it's great on burgers, too.

FOR THE PIMIENTO SPREAD

4 ounces sharp cheddar cheese, grated

4 ounces pepper Jack cheese, grated

¼ cup mayonnaise

One 2-ounce jar of pimientos, drained

2 small sweet gherkin pickles, chopped

2 dashes of hot sauce

FOR THE BURGERS

1 pound ground turkey

3 tablespoons ketchup

Coarse salt and freshly ground black pepper

1 tablespoon canola oil

Toasted bread or buns, for serving

To make the pimiento spread: Combine all of the ingredients in a food processor fitted with the steel blade and pulse several times until well combined. Taste for seasoning and set aside.

To make the burgers: In a medium bowl, combine the turkey with the ketchup and season generously with salt and pepper.

Using your fingers, divide the meat into 4 portions and shape into 4 oval patties. Heat the oil in a skillet over medium-high heat, add the burgers, and cook until no longer pink, about 5 minutes per side. Serve your burgers on toasted bread or buns, smeared with the pimiento spread.

Al Tiramisu Tuscan Duck Stew

From the kitchen of Chef Luigi Diotaiuti

GOOD FOR COMPANY • SERVES 4 TO 6

Chris and I love going to see Chef Luigi at his cozy Al Tiramisu, where he always welcomes us with great gusto and treats us to delicious Italian food that is light and creative. I had the pleasure of the chef treating me to lunch where I first tasted this Tuscan stew and learned about true regional Italian cuisine. Chef Luigi says that this stew is even better served the day after you prepare it. Buon appetito! Serve this accompanied by garlic mashed potatoes, polenta, or braised fennel.

One 4-pound whole duck, skin removed, cut into 10 pieces

2 carrots, trimmed, peeled, and chopped into ¼-inch dice

1 medium onion, chopped

2 medium celery stalks, chopped

2 garlic cloves, minced

5 bay leaves

2 sprigs fresh thyme

1 medium sprig fresh rosemary

One 750-milliliter bottle Chianti wine

2 cups all-purpose flour

2 tablespoons extra-virgin olive oil

2 cups canned crushed tomatoes

Coarse salt and freshly ground black pepper

In a large bowl or plastic container, combine the duck pieces with the carrots, onion, celery, garlic, bay leaves, thyme, and rosemary. Add the wine, cover the bowl with plastic wrap, and marinate in the refrigerator overnight.

Position a rack in the center portion of the oven. Preheat the oven to 350°F.

Using a slotted spoon, remove the vegetables and duck pieces from the marinade and strain the liquid into a large measuring cup and reserve. Dredge the duck pieces in the flour and set aside on a rack or baking sheet.

Heat the oil in a large, heavy-duty Dutch oven or large ovenproof skillet over medium-high heat. Add the dredged duck and cook until slightly browned, about 4 minutes per side. Transfer the duck pieces to a large plate. Add the marinated vegetables to the pot and cook, stirring occasionally and scraping up the brown bits at the bottom, for about 5 minutes. Return the duck pieces and the strained, reserved liquid to the pot and bring to a boil. Reduce the heat and simmer until the liquid has reduced by half, about 25 minutes. Once the liquid has reduced, add the crushed tomatoes, bring to a simmer, and season with salt and pepper to taste.

Transfer the pot to the oven and bake for about 2 hours.

Remove the duck from the pot and discard the bay leaves and herb sprigs. Using a fine-mesh sieve, strain the vegetables from the liquid. Discard the liquid. In a food processor fitted with the steel blade, pulse the vegetables several times to create a chunky sauce. Be careful not to overprocess.

Divide the vegetable gravy among four to six warm plates and top with the duck.

Holiday Lemon Chicken

GOOD FOR COMPANY • SERVES 6

I like to use this recipe for our family gatherings and pair it with my Stuffed Tomatoes with Cucumbers and Feta (page 232). It is pretty when served at a holiday buffet or for a special occasion because you leave the lemons in the baking dish, which add a dash of citrus color to the season.

One 3½-pound chicken, cut into 8 pieces

4 ripe juicy lemons, preferably Meyer lemons

8 peeled garlic cloves

2 teaspoons crushed red pepper flakes

2 tablespoons orange flower honey

4 tablespoons chopped fresh flat-leaf parsley, plus sprigs for garnish

Coarse salt and freshly ground black pepper

Rinse the chicken with cold water and pat dry with paper towels. Place the chicken in a large resealable plastic bag.

Cut the lemons in half, squeeze the lemon juice into a small bowl, and reserve the lemon halves.

Crush two of the garlic cloves and add them to the lemon juice with the red pepper flakes and honey. Stir well to combine and pour the marinade over the chicken in the plastic bag. Refrigerate for 2 hours or up to overnight.

Preheat the oven to 400°F.

Remove the chicken from the bag and discard the marinade. Arrange the chicken in a shallow ovenproof casserole dish, skin side up. Crush the remaining garlic cloves and scatter over the chicken. Place the lemon halves, cut sides down, on top. Bake the chicken for 45 minutes, or until it is golden brown and tender. Stir in the chopped parsley, taste, and if desired season with salt and pepper. Serve garnished with the roasted lemon halves and parsley sprigs.

Chicken in a Pot

Chicken in a pot is a comforting one-pot meal with origins that go back to two cultures: Jewish and French. I like to serve this traditional dish right on the table, and when you crack the seal of the pizza-dough lining the pot, the room fills with the most delicious aromas from the chicken, white turnips, and herbs inside.

One 4½-pound chicken, giblets and wing tips removed

1 tablespoon coarse salt

4 tablespoons extra-virgin olive oil

2 small yellow onions, peeled and quartered, or 16 defrosted frozen pearl onions

2 celery stalks, cut into quarters

6 carrots, trimmed, peeled, and quartered

6 medium garlic cloves, peeled

2 medium white turnips, peeled and cut into 6 wedges, or 6 medium parsnips, peeled and cut into 4 pieces

Freshly ground black pepper

1 tablespoon freshly squeezed lemon, plus a slice of the rind

1 medium fresh rosemary sprig

2 bay leaves

1 cup chicken broth, homemade or store-bought

½ cup dry white wine

Store-bought pizza dough (optional)

Position a rack in the lowest part of the oven. Preheat the oven to 375°F.

Rinse the chicken inside and out with cold water and pat dry with paper towels. Sprinkle the cavity with the salt.

In a large skillet over medium-high heat, warm 2 tablespoons of the oil. Add the onions, celery, carrots, garlic, and turnips and cook, stirring occasionally, until lightly browned, about 5 minutes. Season the vegetable mixture with salt and pepper, then, using a slotted spoon, transfer the mixture to a large Dutch oven.

Return the skillet to the heat, add another tablespoon of the oil, and brown the chicken on all sides, seasoning it with salt and pepper each time you turn it, about 5 minutes per side.

Tuck the chicken in among the vegetables in the pot and tuck the lemon rind, rosemary, and bay leaves in the cavity.

Using a whisk, in a small bowl, combine the broth, wine, lemon juice, and the remaining 1 tablespoon oil. Pour the liquid over the chicken and vegetables in the pot.

Now you have the choice of covering the pot tightly with aluminum foil and a tight-fitting lid or rolling the pizza dough into a long rope with your hands, covering the rim of the pot with the dough, and pressing the lid tightly into the dough. Using a knife, remove any excess

(recipe continues on page 80)

(continued from page 78)

dough from around the lid. Put the pot in the oven and bake the chicken and vegetables for 1 hour.

Remove the pot from the oven and break the seal with a large butter knife. Remove the chicken from the pot, cover loosely with foil, and let rest for 15 minutes, or until ready to carve. Serve the chicken on a large platter with the vegetables and broth, or serve it straight from the pot at the table.

Citrus-Chili Cornish Hens with Lemon Sauce

GOOD FOR COMPANY • SERVES 4

These Cornish hens are another festive dish to serve for large gatherings with family or friends on the holidays. They look beautiful on the plate, served on a bed of Baked Brown Rice (page 201) that cooks in the same oven for about the same time as the hens.

4 small to medium Cornish hens (about 1 pound each)

Coarse salt and freshly ground black pepper

1 cup freshly squeezed lemon juice (about 4 lemons), lemon halves reserved

¾ cup orange marmalade

8 garlic cloves, pressed

2 tablespoons orange blossom honey

2 tablespoons extra-virgin olive oil

1 dried ancho chile

8 tablespoons (1 stick) unsalted butter, melted

Fresh flat-leaf parsley sprigs, for garnish

Rinse the Cornish hens with cold water and pat dry with paper towels. Season generously with salt and pepper and set aside.

Combine the lemon juice, marmalade, pressed garlic, honey, and oil in a bowl large enough to hold the hens. Set the marinade aside.

In a small skillet over medium heat, cook the dried chile for 1 to 2 minutes until softened. Let cool slightly, then remove the stem and seeds and crumble with your fingers into the reserved marinade and mix well. Add the hens to the marinade, breast side down, and coat well on both sides with the sauce. Refrigerate the hens for 6 hours, turning once to coat with the marinade.

Preheat the oven to 425°F.

Add the hens to a baking dish just large enough to hold them firmly together. Pour the marinade through a fine-mesh sieve to remove any bits of seeds or pulp. Pour ½ cup of the marinade over the hens. Put the reserved squeezed lemon halves around the hens and roast for 20 minutes, or until lightly browned.

Melt the butter in a saucepan, add the remaining marinade, bring to a boil, reduce to a simmer, and cook until thickened, about 5 minutes. After 20 minutes of cooking, baste the hens with the butter marinade every 10 minutes until the hens are cooked through, about 45 minutes total cooking time. The hens are done when an instant-read thermometer inserted in the breasts registers 170°F. Transfer the hens to a platter and cover with aluminum foil to keep them warm.

Pour the juices from the baking dish into a fat separator, or skim the fat from the surface of the juices using a large spoon. Arrange the hens on a platter, pour the sauce over, and garnish with the parsley sprigs.

Indian Butter Chicken

BONELESS, SKINLESS • QUICK • STOVETOP • SERVES 4

I was inspired to learn how to make this Indian dish when I was invited by my agent, Michael Psaltis, to a book signing and tasting for Sanjeev Kapoor at a popular Indian restaurant, Indique Heights, in Chevy Chase, Maryland. Chef Sanjeev is a popular TV show host, and is the most celebrated face of Indian cuisine. For a real shortcut, omit the spices and use a jarred Indian Butter Chicken sauce, like Patak's, available at many grocery stores and on the Internet.

1 pound boneless, skinless chicken thighs

2 tablespoons extra-virgin olive oil

1 small onion, diced

1 shallot, finely minced

2 tablespoons unsalted butter

2 teaspoons freshly squeezed lemon juice

2 teaspoons minced garlic

2 teaspoons garam masala spice mixture

1 teaspoon ground ginger

1 teaspoon chili powder

1 teaspoon ground cumin

1 bay leaf

1 cup tomato puree

1 cup half-and-half

¼ cup Greek-style or plain yogurt

Coarse salt and freshly ground black pepper

¼ teaspoon cayenne pepper

Hot cooked rice, for serving (see Jasmine Rice, page 217)

2 tablespoons chopped fresh basil or cilantro leaves, for garnish

1 lime, quartered

Rinse the chicken with cold water and pat dry with paper towels. Cut the chicken into bite-size pieces and set aside.

In a large sauté pan over medium-high heat, warm 1 tablespoon of the oil. Add the onion and shallot and cook, stirring, until soft and translucent, about 5 minutes. Stir in the butter, lemon juice, garlic, 1 teaspoon of the garam masala, the ginger, chili powder, cumin, and bay leaf and cook, stirring, for about 1 minute. Stir in the tomato puree and cook for 2 minutes more. Stir in the half-and-half and the yogurt, reduce the heat to low, and simmer, stirring frequently, for 10 minutes. Do not allow the sauce to boil or it will separate.

While the sauce is cooking, heat another skillet over medium-high heat and add the remaining 1 tablespoon oil.

Season the chicken with salt and pepper, then sprinkle with the cayenne. Add the chicken to the second skillet and cook, turning occasionally, until lightly browned, about 10 minutes. Reduce the heat and add the remaining 1 teaspoon garam masala. Stir a few spoonfuls of the sauce into the chicken mixture and simmer until heated through. Serve over rice, sprinkled with the chopped basil or cilantro, and a squeeze of lime juice.

Nancy's Braised Chicken in Orange Juice

From the kitchen of Nancy Ellison

$ • SERVES 4

Nancy Ellison has lived in both California and Texas and loves the Mexican-style fricassee, pollo a la naranja, *after living in those two regions of the country. She shares with us this simple but elegant braised chicken recipe with a Mexican flair. The recipe is easy to adapt depending on the ingredients used. To give it an Asian twist, use soy sauce, brown sugar, ginger, and garlic. Or make it Middle Eastern by using dried apricots, cinnamon, almonds, and yogurt.*

One 3- to 4-pound chicken, cut into 8 pieces

Coarse salt and freshly ground black pepper

½ cup all-purpose flour

2 tablespoons unsalted butter

2 tablespoons extra-virgin olive oil

½ cup chopped pineapple, fresh or canned

½ cup chopped sliced almonds

½ cup chopped raisins

Pinch of ground cinnamon

Pinch of ground cloves

2 cups orange juice

Orange and avocado slices, for garnish

Note: *For a thicker sauce, transfer the chicken after 45 minutes to a large platter and cover with aluminum foil. Increase the heat and whisk the sauce in the skillet until thickened, about 3 minutes.*

Rinse the chicken with cold water and pat dry with paper towels. Place the chicken on a baking sheet and season with salt and pepper. Cover loosely with aluminum foil. Set aside.

Pour the flour into a shallow dish such as a pie plate. Coat the chicken pieces in the flour, shaking off any excess flour. Put the chicken on a rack or baking sheet.

In a large skillet over medium-low heat, melt the butter with the oil. Add the coated chicken to the skillet and brown the chicken on each side, about 4 minutes per side, working in batches, if needed.

In a small bowl, combine the pineapple, almonds, raisins, cinnamon, and cloves. When the chicken has browned, add the orange juice and the fruit-spice mixture to the skillet and bring to a boil. Reduce the heat to medium-low, cover, and simmer until the chicken is cooked through, about 45 minutes.

Remove the lid and continue to cook until the sauce has reduced and thickened, about 15 minutes more. Taste the sauce and adjust the seasoning with salt and pepper, if needed. Serve the chicken on a wide-rimmed platter with the sauce, garnished with the orange and avocado slices.

Spring

In the spring, Washington transforms into a glorious city.
The famous cherry blossom trees ring the monuments downtown. Daffodils decorate roadways in the parks. It is the season when we toss off our winter coats and open the windows to enjoy the light warm breezes. Newly green pastures are filled with little white lambs, yellow chicks, pink piglets, and young calves. Farmers' markets reopen and are abundant with tender stalks of asparagus and wild morels. It is opening day for the Nationals baseball team. In April, we celebrate Easter and Passover, the time of rebirth. May is the running of the Preakness in Maryland and the Gold Cup steeplechase race in Virginia. This "Spring" chapter offers recipes that use the much welcomed fresh produce and young chickens that come with the new season.

The Chicken Scaloppine with Sugar Snap Peas, Asparagus, and Lemon Salad is a light dish. Steamed fresh sugar snap peas and asparagus are tossed with a lemon dressing and spooned on top of thin, sautéed chicken paillards that cook in minutes. Another favorite in our house comes from Frank Pellegrino, chef and owner of the fabulous Rao's restaurant in New York City. It is his mom's recipe. Ida's Baked Chicken calls for fresh tender peas, carrots, and potatoes that are all roasted in one pan with a delicious Italian flair.

I enjoy serving a large buffet for our Easter supper, which includes a roasted leg of lamb, Spring Chicken Roll-Ups with Lemon Sauce, blanched spring asparagus, Gruyère Cheese au Gratin Potatoes, and Sweet-and-Sour Spring Carrots (see "Sides" chapter). Adding the chicken roll-ups to the menu adds a flavorful alternative to the lamb, and the recipe can be prepared the day prior to our feast. My potato gratin is a family favorite that I have been making since I first learned to cook. By using cheese and less cream, you have a golden casserole that makes your Easter dinner delicious without doing quite so much damage to your diet. When I make the baby carrots, I peel and remove the green tops, toss the carrots in red wine vinegar and a little sugar, then cook them in the oven on high heat for a short period of time until they are tender. This is a recipe that is simple to keep warm while carving your lamb.

When packing a tailgate picnic for a day at the May races (or a few years ago, for one of the boys' baseball games), I always keep the temperature in mind and how the picnic lunch will hold for an afternoon of outdoor fun. That is when I often pack fried

top left: Sarah with the Easter Bunny, 2011. top right: Peter, Chris, and Andrew at the Masters, 2011. below: Spring Gold Cup Races. Photo by Isabel Kurek. right: Chef Art Smith with renowned artist Jesus Salgueiro

chicken and a light mayonnaise vinegar slaw. For dessert, I make Chris's favorite "four-kinds-of-chips" cookies or pack some luscious ripe large strawberries for dipping in powdered sugar.

Art Smith, chef and owner of three restaurants across the country, shares his recipe for crispy fried chicken from his restaurant here in Washington, Art and Soul. He soaks the chicken overnight in a brine of kosher salt and water, strains the brine off, then resoaks the chicken in a spicy buttermilk bath before dusting it in flour loaded with more herbs and spices just prior to frying it in a cast-iron skillet.

My friend Ann Free and her husband Jim are from the South. When I was looking for the perfect coleslaw recipe, she suggested one that her family has made for generations, which I have used as an inspiration for creating my Vinegar Slaw (see "Sides" chapter).

Spring is a time of renewal, with more entertaining and activities outside. I hope these dishes will become part of your family traditions during this very special season.

Quick Turkey and Green Bean Stir-Fry

QUICK • FAMILY FAVORITE • SERVES 4

This is the recipe that our daughter Sarah craved in high school when she had limited time to eat between her school work and drama classes. Even though we are empty nesters now, this is still one of our favorites.

3 tablespoons canola oil

One 2-inch piece of peeled fresh ginger, grated

4 garlic cloves, thinly sliced

1 pound ground turkey

Coarse salt and freshly ground black pepper

3 tablespoons soy sauce

3 tablespoons Japanese mirin

1 pound green beans, trimmed and cut in half

2 cups loosely packed fresh basil leaves

¼ cup coarsely chopped salted peanuts

In a large skillet over medium-high heat, warm 2 tablespoons of the oil until shimmering. Add the ginger and garlic and stir-fry until fragrant, about 30 seconds. Add the turkey, season with salt and pepper, and cook, stirring the meat to break it up, for about 5 minutes. Add the soy sauce and mirin and cook for 1 minute more.

Transfer the meat mixture to a bowl and wipe out the skillet with paper towels.

Return the skillet to the stovetop over medium heat, add the remaining 1 tablespoon oil, and heat until shimmering. Add the green beans and stir-fry until crisp-tender and blackened in spots, about 5 minutes. Remove the skillet from the heat, return the turkey mixture to the skillet, cook briefly to reheat, and toss in the basil leaves. Serve immediately on large warm plates, garnished with the salted peanuts.

Spring Chicken Roll-Ups with Lemon Sauce

BONELESS, SKINLESS • GOOD FOR COMPANY • SERVES 4

This is a dish I like to serve for Easter since it is spring chicken stuffed with the bounty of the season—asparagus. The recipe is easy to make in advance and serve at room temperature for a buffet.

12 thin asparagus spears, woody stem ends trimmed

2 boneless, skinless chicken breasts

Coarse salt and freshly ground black pepper

4 slices provolone cheese

1 tablespoon extra-virgin olive oil

2 tablespoons unsalted butter

2 tablespoons all-purpose flour

1 cup dry white wine

1 tablespoon Dijon mustard

¼ cup chopped fresh flat-leaf parsley

Finely grated zest and juice of ½ lemon

Pinch of ground white pepper

Preheat the oven to 350°F.

Blanch the asparagus in a large pot of salted boiling water for about 2 minutes. Rinse under cold running water, drain, and pat dry with paper towels.

Rinse the chicken breasts with cold water and pat dry with paper towels. Cut the chicken breasts in half horizontally and pound between 2 pieces of plastic wrap to create 4 thin cutlets, each about ¼ inch thick. Season the cutlets on both sides with salt and black pepper. Cover a cutlet with a slice of the cheese. Place 3 asparagus spears toward the end of each cutlet. Wrap and roll the chicken and cheese around the asparagus. Place on a plate, seam side down, and repeat the procedure with the remaining cutlets.

In a skillet over medium-high heat, warm the oil. Place the chicken roll-ups, seam side down, in the skillet. Brown the roll-ups on all sides, about 3 minutes. Transfer the cooked roll-ups to an ovenproof baking dish that is large enough to hold them. Bake for 20 minutes until cooked through and golden.

Meanwhile, add the butter to the skillet. Whisk in the flour and cook off the raw taste, for about 1 minute. Add the wine and stir to combine. Add the mustard and scrape up any brown bits from the bottom of the skillet. Simmer for several minutes until the sauce begins to thicken. Reduce the heat to low, add the parsley, lemon zest, and lemon juice and cook until heated through. Taste for seasoning and add additional salt, if needed, and white pepper to taste.

Tip: *You can make the raw roll-ups and refrigerate overnight until ready to bake.*

When the roll-ups have finished cooking, remove them from the oven and let stand for 5 minutes. Cut each roll-up into 3 pieces to make pinwheels and transfer to a serving platter. Spoon the sauce over the top and serve immediately.

Quick Chicken Cordon Bleu

BONELESS, SKINLESS • QUICK • SERVES 4

Here is a classic French chicken preparation that is traditionally made with ham. Here I've used prosciutto because our family prefers it. Slice the chicken and roll into pinwheels for a great presentation.

Nonstick cooking spray

4 boneless, skinless chicken breasts

¼ teaspoon coarse salt

¼ teaspoon freshly ground black pepper

4 pieces Swiss cheese

4 slices prosciutto

½ cup seasoned dried bread crumbs or panko bread crumbs

4 tablespoons (½ stick) unsalted butter, melted

Preheat the oven to 350°F. Coat a baking sheet with nonstick cooking spray.

Rinse the chicken breasts with cold water and pat dry with paper towels. Trim off any excess fat. Remove the tender (filet) and reserve for later use; it will make the breast more uniform when pounded. Place each breast between 2 pieces of plastic wrap and, using the flat side of a meat mallet, pound each breast to a thickness of about ¼ inch. Place the cutlets on a flat work surface and season generously with the salt and pepper. Place 1 slice of the cheese and prosciutto on top of each cutlet. Roll up each breast like a jelly roll, securing with a toothpick through the middle, if needed.

Put the bread crumbs in a medium bowl. Add the stuffed breasts, one by one, to the bowl and coat with the bread crumbs, gently pressing the bread crumbs onto the chicken so that they adhere. Transfer the chicken breasts to the prepared baking sheet and let stand for 15 minutes.

Drizzle the melted butter over the chicken and bake for 20 to 30 minutes until golden and the chicken is no longer pink. Allow to rest 5 minutes before serving.

Fajita Chicken Packets

BONELESS, SKINLESS • QUICK • SERVES 4

Looking for an alternative to a taco dinner? Try these individual Mexican packets that have all the flavors of a traditional fajita dinner. If you don't have parchment paper, just use aluminum foil to make the packets. Serve with your favorite salsa, guacamole, and chips.

½ cup chopped fresh cilantro

2 tablespoons freshly squeezed lime juice (about 2 small limes)

2 garlic cloves, minced

1 teaspoon dried oregano

3 teaspoons extra-virgin olive oil

4 boneless, skinless chicken breasts

¼ teaspoon coarse salt

¼ teaspoon freshly ground black pepper

1 large sweet onion, halved and sliced into ¼-inch-thick half-moons (about 2 cups)

1 large red bell pepper, seeded and cut into ¼-inch strips (about 2 cups)

1 tablespoon chopped canned green chilies

One 15-ounce can corn kernels, drained

One 15-ounce can black beans, rinsed and drained

Salsa, guacamole, and chips, for serving

Preheat the oven to 425°F.

In a food processor fitted with the steel blade, process the cilantro, lime juice, garlic, oregano, and 1½ teaspoons of the olive oil by pulsing for 2 minutes until it forms a paste.

Rinse the chicken breasts with cold water and pat dry with paper towels. Lightly season the chicken breasts with salt and pepper on both sides. Place each chicken breast between 2 pieces of plastic wrap. Using the flat side of a meat mallet, pound each evenly to create thin cutlets, each about ¼ inch thick. Rub each cutlet with the cilantro-lime paste, coating evenly on top.

In a large skillet over high heat, warm 1 teaspoon of the oil and swirl in the skillet to coat it evenly. Add the onion and bell pepper and cook, stirring constantly, until slightly soft and the onions are golden, 3 minutes. Set aside.

Cut out four 12 × 17-inch pieces of parchment paper, fold each in half crosswise to form a crease, then open each up.

Divide the onions and peppers roughly into fourths in the skillet. Place one-fourth of the onion and pepper mixture on the bottom of each piece of parchment paper, then add ¼ teaspoon of the chopped chilies, one-fourth of the corn kernels (about ⅓ cup), and one-fourth of the beans. Put the chicken breast on top of the beans and drizzle with the remaining oil. Fold the parchment paper over the ingredients, make overlapping pleats around the outside edge to seal, then tuck the ends under.

Arrange the packets on a large baking sheet, making sure not to crowd the baking sheet. Bake in the oven for 25 to 30 minutes until the chicken is no longer pink. Serve the packets on warm individual plates along with salsa, guacamole, and chips.

Red Curry Chicken with Vegetables

From the kitchen of Chantima Suka

BONELESS, SKINLESS • VEGGIE • SERVES 4

Chantima, aka Jim, makes a mean Chicken Curry in which she uses red curry paste and coconut combined with fish sauce and topped off with Thai basil!

2 boneless, skinless chicken breasts

2 tablespoons vegetable oil

One 13.4-ounce can coconut milk

½ cup red curry paste (preferably Maesri brand)

2½ cups chicken broth, homemade or store-bought, or water

One 20-ounce can sliced bamboo shoots packed in water, drained

2 tablespoons palm sugar, or substitute light brown sugar

2 to 4 teaspoons fish sauce, or to taste

1 medium red bell pepper, seeded and sliced in ¼-inch pieces (about 1 cup)

½ cup fresh Thai basil leaves

Hot cooked basmati rice or Jasmine Rice (page 217), for serving

Rinse the chicken with cold water and pat dry with paper towels.

In a skillet over medium-high heat, warm 1 tablespoon of the oil and swirl the pan to coat. Add the chicken breasts and cook until golden, but still pink inside and not cooked through, 3 to 4 minutes per side. Transfer to a cutting board and, when cool enough to handle, slice on the diagonal into ½-inch pieces and set aside.

Meanwhile, add ¾ cup of the coconut milk to a large saucepan and set over medium-high heat. Add the red curry paste, stir well to combine, and cook for about 5 minutes. Add the reserved chicken slices, the broth, bamboo shoots, and the remaining coconut milk and cook for about 1 minute. Add the sugar, fish sauce to taste (every brand is different in salt content), and bell peppers and continue to cook until the chicken is cooked through, 10 to 15 minutes more.

Remove the skillet from the heat, taste, and adjust the seasoning with more sugar or fish sauce, if needed. Tear the basil with your fingers and sprinkle it on top. Serve the curry in warm bowls over cooked basmati or jasmine rice.

Spring Chicken with Artichokes and Fennel

$ • SERVES 4

I love this dish since it is all prepared in one skillet and yet has the flavors of a more involved dish that requires a long bake in the oven. Remember to start with a preheated skillet and don't be tempted to move the chicken around as it browns.

One 4-pound chicken, cut into 10 pieces

Coarse salt and freshly ground black pepper

1 tablespoon extra-virgin olive oil

1 fennel bulb, trimmed and cut into ¼-inch wedges (about 2 cups), ¼ cup chopped fronds reserved

1 small red onion, cut into ½-inch wedges (about 2 cups)

2 cups chicken broth, homemade or store-bought

One 15-ounce can water-packed whole artichoke hearts, drained

1 bay leaf

1 tablespoon sherry vinegar

3 tablespoons coarsely chopped fresh flat-leaf parsley

Rinse the chicken pieces with cold water and pat dry with paper towels. Season both sides of the chicken pieces with salt and pepper.

In a large skillet over high heat, warm the oil and swirl to evenly coat the skillet. Add the chicken, working in batches if necessary, to avoid overcrowding the skillet, and brown on all sides, 8 to 10 minutes total. Transfer the chicken to a plate.

Pour off all but 1 tablespoon of the fat from the skillet, reduce the heat to medium-high, add the fennel and onions wedges, and cook, stirring occasionally, until browned, about 5 minutes more.

Return the chicken to the skillet and add the broth, artichokes, and bay leaf. Reduce the heat to a simmer, cover, and continue to cook until the chicken is cooked through, about 30 minutes.

Transfer the chicken and vegetables to a large platter. Discard the bay leaf. Over medium-high heat, reduce the liquid in the skillet to ½ cup.

Remove the skillet from the heat, add the vinegar, and stir well to combine the liquids. Taste and adjust the seasoning, if necessary. Pour the sauce over the chicken and vegetables on the platter and top with the reserved chopped fennel fronds and parsley.

Ida's Baked Chicken

From Rao's: Recipes from the Neighborhood

FAMILY FAVORITE • GOOD FOR COMPANY • SERVES 4

Frank Pellegrino says that his mother Ida was always worried about having enough food on the table, so on Sundays, along with the macaroni and all the Sunday gravy meat, she would also make a baked chicken. There was enough for a block party!

One 3-pound chicken, cut into 12 pieces

¼ cup freshly grated Pecorino Romano cheese

¼ cup chopped fresh flat-leaf parsley

2 teaspoons coarse salt

¾ teaspoon freshly ground black pepper

½ teaspoon garlic powder

½ cup extra-virgin olive oil, plus additional for drizzling

1 cup plain dried bread crumbs

3 baking potatoes, peeled and cut into eighths

1 cup medium peeled and sliced carrots

1 cup peas, drained if canned, defrosted if frozen

Preheat the oven to 375°F.

Rinse the chicken pieces with cold water and pat dry with paper towels. Put the chicken in a large bowl and add the cheese, parsley, 1 teaspoon of the salt, ½ teaspoon of the pepper, and the garlic powder. Add the oil and mix well until the chicken is well coated and moist. Put the bread crumbs in a bowl, add the chicken pieces, and coat with the bread crumbs. Set aside.

In a separate bowl, toss the potatoes with the remaining 1 teaspoon salt and ¼ teaspoon pepper and drizzle with some oil to coat. Spread a thin layer of the oil on the bottom of a roasting pan large enough to hold the chicken and potatoes. Arrange the chicken, skin side down, in the pan. Scatter the potatoes around the chicken and drizzle with oil. Cover and bake for 30 minutes. Reduce the heat to 350°F, stir the chicken and potatoes and bake, uncovered, for 45 minutes more.

Meanwhile, parboil the carrots in boiling water for 4 to 5 minutes, drain, and season with salt. Parboil the peas, if using fresh peas, and drain. Combine the carrots and peas. If you are using frozen peas, season with ½ teaspoon salt and add them 10 minutes before the chicken is done.

Transfer the chicken and vegetables to a platter and serve.

Pantry Chicken Saté with Peanut Sauce

BONELESS, SKINLESS • GRILL • SERVES 4 TO 6

When spring fever hits and I move outdoors and fire up the grill, this is one of my favorites! For a spring dinner party, I often make smaller skewers and serve them as cocktail nibbles.

If using a store-bought sweetened creamy peanut butter, then it's not necessary to add the brown sugar to the sauce.

FOR THE SATÉ

3 pounds boneless, skinless chicken breasts

Nonstick cooking spray

4½ tablespoons soy sauce

2 tablespoons light brown sugar

4 garlic cloves, minced

4 teaspoons peeled and grated fresh ginger

2 teaspoons finely grated lime zest

½ teaspoon crushed red pepper flakes

Sixteen 8-inch skewers (see Tip)

FOR THE DIPPING SAUCE

6 tablespoons unsweetened creamy peanut butter

3½ tablespoons soy sauce

3 garlic cloves, minced

3 tablespoons light brown sugar

3 tablespoons freshly squeezed lime juice

¾ teaspoon crushed red pepper flakes

Rinse the chicken with cool water and pat dry with paper towels. Cut the chicken breasts lengthwise into 16 total pieces, Coat the grill rack with nonstick cooking spray. Preheat the grill to medium-high heat (450°F–500°F).

To prepare the saté: In a bowl, combine the soy sauce, brown sugar, garlic, ginger, lime zest, and red pepper flakes. Add the chicken strips and toss well to coat. Let stand for 10 minutes or overnight in the refrigerator, tightly covered.

To prepare the dipping sauce: In a bowl, combine the peanut butter, soy sauce, garlic, brown sugar, lime juice, and red pepper flakes and stir until the sugar dissolves.

Thread the chicken strips onto the skewers. Place the skewers on the grill rack and grill each side for about 5 minutes, or until cooked through. Serve the chicken saté on a large platter along with the dipping sauce.

> **Tip:** *Bamboo skewers, an alternative to metal skewers, get hot quickly and can burn. To help prevent this, place the skewers in a baking dish or pan, cover with warm water, and soak for at least 30 minutes prior to use.*

Chicken Scaloppine with Sugar Snap Peas, Asparagus, and Lemon Salad

BONELESS, SKINLESS • SERVES 6

If you don't have time to pound your chicken breasts to make the scaloppine, then purchase chicken cutlets at your market as a shortcut. The lemon-dressed vegetable salad on top of the warm chicken is a treat.

FOR THE SALAD

1 pound sugar snap peas

2 cups asparagus, cut into 1-inch pieces

2½ tablespoons extra-virgin olive oil

1½ tablespoons freshly squeezed lemon juice

1 tablespoon chopped fresh mint

1 teaspoon finely grated lemon zest

FOR THE CHICKEN SCALOPPINE

6 boneless, skinless chicken breasts (about 6 ounces each)

Coarse salt and freshly ground black pepper

3 teaspoons canola oil

1 cup chicken broth, homemade or store-bought

⅓ cup dry white wine

1 tablespoon butter

6 lemon wedges, for serving

To begin making the salad: Fill a pot with several inches of boiling water and fit it with a steamer basket. Steam the sugar snap peas and asparagus, covered, until crisp-tender, about 4 minutes. Rinse the vegetables quickly with cold water, drain, and chill in the refrigerator.

To make the chicken scaloppine: Rinse the chicken with cold water and pat dry with paper towels.

Place each chicken breast between 2 sheets of plastic wrap and, using the flat side of a meat mallet, pound to a thickness of about ¼ inch. Season the chicken with salt and pepper.

In a nonstick skillet over medium-high heat, warm the oil. Working in 3 batches, add the chicken to the pan. Cook for 2 minutes on each side, or until cooked through. Transfer the chicken to a platter and cover loosely with aluminum foil to keep it warm. Repeat the procedure twice more to cook the remaining two batches of chicken. As you cook the chicken, transfer it to the platter and keep it warm.

Add the broth and wine to the skillet and bring to a boil, scraping up any brown bits from the bottom of the skillet. Simmer the sauce until reduced to about ½ cup. Whisk in the butter. Return the chicken breasts to the skillet and coat with the sauce.

(recipe continues on page 99)

(continued from page 96)

To finish the salad: In a small bowl, combine the olive oil, lemon juice, mint, and lemon zest until combined. Toss the steamed, chilled vegetables with the dressing. Serve the salad atop the chicken and garnish with the lemon wedges.

Chicken and Cashews in Lettuce Cups

QUICK • STOVETOP • SERVES 6

This is a quick recipe I like to make for a satisfying supper on time-sensitive days, and especially when I have Asian Noodles (page 200) and Pickled Cucumbers (page 227) in the refrigerator to serve on the side.

3 tablespoons low-sodium soy sauce

3 tablespoons orange blossom honey

2 tablespoons canola oil

1½ pounds ground chicken

Coarse salt and freshly ground black pepper

3 garlic cloves, finely chopped

2 tablespoons peeled and grated fresh ginger

2 tablespoons light brown sugar

1 bunch scallions, trimmed and sliced on the diagonal

One 8-ounce can water chestnuts, rinsed and drained

1 cup unsalted, roasted cashews

1 head Boston or Bibb lettuce, well washed, leaves separated

In a small bowl, whisk together the soy sauce and honey and set aside.

In a large skillet over medium heat, warm the oil. Add the ground chicken, season with salt and pepper, and cook, stirring to break up the meat, until it begins to brown, about 5 minutes. Reduce the heat to medium and stir in the garlic, ginger, and brown sugar. Add the scallions and cook for 2 minutes more.

Stir in the water chestnuts and the soy-honey mixture and continue to cook until the chicken is cooked through, about 3 minutes more. Transfer the chicken to a serving bowl and sprinkle with the cashews. Place the lettuce leaves on a platter next to the bowl of chicken and allow the diners to fill their own lettuce leaves.

Sesame Chicken with Edamame

BONELESS, SKINLESS • SERVES 4

Flavorful golden, sesame-coated chicken served over a bed of sticky brown rice makes for a perfect weeknight dinner.

1½ pounds boneless, skinless chicken breasts

3 tablespoons soy sauce

4 teaspoons sesame oil

2 teaspoons honey

2 tablespoons plus 2 teaspoons canola oil

2 scallions, thinly sliced

1 tablespoon peeled and grated fresh ginger

3 garlic cloves, minced

1 cup chicken broth, homemade or store-bought

3 tablespoons sugar

1 tablespoon cornstarch

1 tablespoon rice vinegar

1 teaspoon Thai chili paste

4 cups shelled edamame

2 tablespoons toasted sesame seeds

Hot cooked brown rice (optional), for serving

Rinse the chicken with cold water and pat dry with paper towels. Cut into ¾-inch chunks and set aside.

In a large bowl, whisk 1½ tablespoons of the soy sauce with 2 teaspoons of the sesame oil and the honey. Add the chicken and stir to coat with the marinade. Marinate for 20 minutes or refrigerate for up to 2 hours.

In a nonstick skillet over medium-high heat, warm 2 tablespoons of the canola oil. Remove the chicken from the marinade using a slotted spoon. Discard the marinade. Cook the chicken in 2 batches, stirring occasionally, until browned, 3 to 5 minutes. Transfer the chicken to a plate, and wipe out the skillet with paper towels.

Heat the remaining 2 teaspoons canola oil in the skillet. Add the scallions, reserving some of the green parts for garnish. Add the ginger and garlic and cook, stirring, for 1 minute.

In a bowl, whisk together the broth, sugar, cornstarch, vinegar, chili paste, and the remaining 1½ tablespoons soy sauce. Add to the skillet and cook, stirring, until thickened, 3 to 4 minutes. Stir in the remaining 2 teaspoons sesame oil.

Meanwhile, cook the edamame in a steamer basket, set over a pot with a few inches of boiling water until crisp-tender, 2 to 3 minutes.

Return the chicken to the skillet with the sauce and heat through. Add the edamame, the toasted sesame seeds, and the reserved scallions and toss to combine. Serve hot on a bed of sticky brown rice, if desired.

Greek Stuffed Chicken Breasts

BONELESS, SKINLESS • QUICK • SERVES 8

I love this combination of ingredients that captures the flavors of Greece—olives, feta, and oregano. And this dish offers all that and more for a scrumptious baked dinner in under 30 minutes. Add the Lemon Orzo (page 222) or Greek-Style Lima Beans (page 216) to round out the meal.

3½ pounds boneless, skinless whole chicken breasts (8)

Coarse salt and freshly ground black pepper

6 tablespoons extra-virgin olive oil

4 tablespoons (½ stick) unsalted butter

6 cups diced tomatoes, drained

4 cups sliced mixed mushrooms (about 16 ounces)

½ cup chopped Kalamata olives

1 large white onion, chopped (about 2 cups)

⅔ cup crumbled feta cheese

2 tablespoons dried oregano

Fresh flat-leaf parsley sprigs, for garnish

Preheat the oven to 450°F.

Rinse the chicken breasts with cold water and pat dry with paper towels. Place each chicken breast between 2 sheets of plastic wrap. Pound with the flat side of a meat mallet to a thickness of ¼ inch. Season each side with salt and pepper and transfer to a large roasting pan.

In a large skillet over medium-high heat, warm the oil and butter. When the butter has melted, add the tomatoes, mushrooms, olives, and onion and cook, stirring occasionally, until the mushrooms have softened and released some of their liquid, 8 to 10 minutes. Remove from the heat and stir in the cheese and oregano.

Spread 4 to 5 tablespoons of the filling into a log down the center of each piece of chicken, then roll each up jelly-roll style. Keep the filling in place by positioning each completed roll, seam side down, in a 13 × 9-inch baking dish, arranging the rolls about 2 inches apart. Or secure each roll with a toothpick, if needed. Scatter the remaining filling mixture around the chicken in the dish.

Roast for 15 minutes, then reduce the heat to 400°F and roast for 15 to 20 minutes more. Let rest for 10 minutes, loosely covered with aluminum foil. Slice the chicken rolls crosswise and transfer to a large platter and garnish with parsley sprigs.

Art and Soul Fried Chicken

From the kitchen of Chef Art Smith

Chef Art Smith was a Power Player of the Week on Chris's show, Fox News Sunday, *for the charity he founded, Common Threads. For my birthday, Chris surprised me by taking me to Art's restaurant, Art and Soul, in Washington, D.C., to meet and dine with the chef. Art has been a favorite person of mine ever since; I love his huge heart and warm personality. Several years ago, we were honored to witness his marriage to renowned artist Jesus Salgueiro. Here is Art's famous fried chicken recipe. Enjoy!*

½ cup plus 1 teaspoon coarse salt

4 quarts cold water

One 4-pound chicken, cut into 8 pieces

1 quart buttermilk

2 tablespoons hot sauce

2 cups all-purpose flour

1 tablespoon baking powder

1½ teaspoons garlic powder

1½ teaspoons Chesapeake Bay seasoning

1 teaspoon cayenne pepper

1 teaspoon freshly ground black pepper

Vegetable oil for frying

In a large, pot, dissolve ½ cup of the salt in the water. Submerge the chicken pieces in the brine and refrigerate overnight. The next day, drain the chicken and rinse with cold water. Rinse out the pot, return the chicken to the pot, add the buttermilk and hot sauce, and refrigerate for 8 hours or overnight.

In a shallow bowl, whisk together the flour, baking powder, garlic powder, Chesapeake Bay seasoning, cayenne, black pepper, and the remaining 1 teaspoon salt.

Remove the chicken from the buttermilk marinade, shaking off any excess. Dredge the chicken pieces in the flour mixture, dip back into the buttermilk, then coat again with the flour mixture.

Meanwhile, in a large cast-iron skillet, heat 1 inch of oil to 375°F. Fry the chicken in batches until golden brown and cooked through, about 6 minutes per side. Drain on paper towels and serve.

Quick Chicken and Vegetable Quiche

ROTISSERIE CHICKEN • VEGGIE • SERVES 6

Using a store-bought refrigerated pie crust really cuts down the time needed to prepare this golden quiche filled with caramelized onions and tender asparagus. To create a vegetarian supper, just omit the chicken or make the pie half and half for a creative way to satisfy all your family's dietary needs.

1 refrigerated pie crust

2 tablespoons extra-virgin olive oil

1 large yellow onion, thinly sliced

1 teaspoon coarse salt

½ cup fresh asparagus, tough woody stems snapped off and discarded, cut into ½-inch pieces

1½ cups cooked shredded chicken, from a store-bought rotisserie chicken or leftover roasted chicken

5 large eggs, beaten

¾ cup whole milk

Freshly ground black pepper

1 cup Gruyère or Emmenthal Swiss cheese, shredded

Preheat the oven to 425°F.

Roll out the refrigerated pie crust and line a 9- or 10-inch pie or quiche plate. Prick the dough all over with the tines of a fork and crimp the edges between your thumb and forefinger so they form a pattern along the top edge of the plate. Place a piece of aluminum foil into the tart shell and weight with pie weights, uncooked rice, or dried beans. Prebake the shell until crisp, 10 to 12 minutes.

Meanwhile, heat the oil in a large skillet over medium heat. Add the onions and sprinkle with the salt. Cook, stirring, until the onions are wilted and translucent, about 5 minutes. Reduce the heat and continue to cook, stirring occasionally, until the onions have softened completely and are lightly caramelized, another 20 minutes. Add the asparagus to the skillet and toss until slightly cooked, about 3 minutes. Add the chicken and toss together with the asparagus and onions until heated through, about 3 minutes.

Reduce the oven temperature to 375°F.

In a large measuring cup, whisk the eggs and milk together and season with salt and pepper.

(recipe continues on page 106)

(continued from page 105)

Place the prebaked pie crust on a baking sheet to prevent any egg mixture from spilling into the oven and place the meat-vegetable mixture into the crust, top with grated cheese, and then carefully pour over the egg-milk mixture. Bake for 35 minutes, or until the top begins to brown and the custard is almost set in the middle. Allow to stand for 10 minutes before slicing and serving.

Low-Fat Chicken Tagine with Parsnip Puree

ONE POT • SERVES 4

I like to serve this vegetable-packed, low-calorie chicken tagine ladled on top of my Parsnip Puree (page 226) in large, wide-rimmed bowls, topped with tender green peas.

One 4-pound chicken, cut up; thigh and drumsticks separated; breasts, halved; skin removed; wing tips, trimmed

Coarse salt and freshly ground black pepper

½ teaspoon saffron threads, crumbled

½ teaspoon ground ginger

½ teaspoon ground coriander

½ teaspoon ground cumin

½ teaspoon hot paprika

¼ teaspoon ground turmeric

1 medium white onion, chopped

1½ cups chicken broth, homemade or store-bought

2 medium tomatoes, cut into eighths

Rinse the chicken with cold water, and pat dry with paper towels. Place the chicken pieces on a plate and season with salt and pepper.

In a small bowl, mix together the saffron threads with the ginger, coriander, cumin, paprika, and turmeric.

In a large, ovenproof enameled pot, combine the chicken pieces with the chopped onion and broth and bring to a boil. Add the spice mixture, reduce the heat, cover, and simmer, turning occasionally, for about 25 minutes. Transfer the breasts to a plate and cover loosely with aluminum foil to keep them warm.

Continue to simmer the thighs, drumsticks, and wings, covered, for 10 minutes more. Add the tomatoes, artichoke hearts, and preserved lemon zest and continue to simmer, uncovered, for 3 minutes more. Season with salt and pepper to taste. Add the peas.

One 14-ounce can whole
    artichoke hearts, drained,
    halved

¼ preserved lemon, zest only,
    minced

1½ cups frozen petite peas,
    defrosted

Parsnip Puree (page 226),
    for serving

Return the chicken breasts to the pot and simmer
gently, turning a few times until heated through, about
2 minutes. Serve the tagine in wide-rimmed, shallow
bowls, ladled over a mound of parsnip puree.

Make Ahead: *The
chicken tagine can be covered
tightly and refrigerated
overnight. Reheat gently
before serving.*

Note: *Preserved lemons are a Moroccan staple made
from lemons that have been cured in lemon juice and salt.
Look for them in the gourmet food aisle or on the Internet.*

Summer

Since the days are hot and humid in Washington, summer
evenings are the times we spend outdoors—eating crabs, sitting in backyards enjoying
barbecues, and preparing picnic baskets packed with fried chicken. On the Fourth
of July at the National Mall, there is a fireworks show, a splendid sight that we enjoy
in a festive gathering of family and friends to celebrate the country's birthday. Great
American food is part of the celebration: spicy and sweet, hot and cold, grilled steaks,
hot dogs, sweet tea and lemonade, corn and coleslaw, summer berries, fruit pies,
cobblers, and so much more.

When the weather permits, I like to move outdoors to grill and prepare dishes like
my Grilled Pesto Chicken. You simply marinate chicken breasts in store-bought pesto
(or make your own from fresh summer basil), then grill the breasts and serve on top of
grilled polenta rounds topped with a warm, cooked fresh cherry tomato sauce.

When I prepare a supper on the grill, I often use the opportunity to grill extra
chicken for other meals. I just lightly rub chicken breasts with olive oil, grill until done,
and then refrigerate them until I am ready to use them for a new meal. Often I use
the extra chicken to make my Grilled Chicken and Herbed Farfalle Pasta Salad, which
makes a delicious lunch or is great to have on hand in the refrigerator for hot days
when you don't want to cook.

To enjoy the outdoor taste indoors, I like to use the stovetop and my oven to make
summer classics like Stovetop Summer Chicken and Basted Barbecue Chicken with
Carolina-Style Barbecue Sauce. To prepare the stovetop chicken, you simply butterfly a
young bird by removing the backbone (or have your butcher do it for you), rub it with
olive oil to coat, and cook it in a cast-iron skillet for under an hour with fresh garlic and
herbs. The chicken is crisp on the outside and moist and juicy on the inside.

I make the Carolina-Style Barbecue Sauce in June and use it all summer long,
keeping a supply in the refrigerator. When I wanted to learn how to make a lighter style
barbecue sauce from the Carolinas, I visited my girlfriend Ann Free who is from there.
And sure enough, out came several books from the Junior League to the Presbyterian
Church Ladies Auxiliaries. This recipe is inspired by an especially tasty-looking one from
300 Years of Carolina Cooking. The recipe makes about 8 cups, a lot more sauce than you'll
need for the Basted Barbecue Chicken recipe, but I often double the recipe for the sauce.

Peter grilling at his home in Bridgehampton, Summer 2011.

above: Sarah, Remick, Catherine, and me, Fourth of July weekend, 2011.
right: "Girlfriends" : Shannon, Juliette, and Catherine

It lasts for up to 3 months and makes a perfect hostess gift, when placed in Mason jars with your own printed label and with my slow-basted chicken recipe attached.

The sauce base is vinegar with sugar, onions, and tons of lemon for a zesty taste. Also in this "Summer" chapter, I share two kinds of baked fried chicken. The first is my mom's Herbed Buttermilk "Not-Fried" Chicken. She used crushed cornflakes for her recipe, but I have taken it a step further by creating an herb-buttermilk bath that you soak the chicken in overnight, which adds even more flavor.

Chef Art Smith's Southern Oven "Unfried" Chicken recipe uses buttermilk, too, but he adds Louisiana hot sauce and uses skinless chicken breasts covered with whole-wheat panko bread crumbs to make his recipe healthier. This is one of Chef Art's signature dishes at Lyfe Kitchen, his new restaurant in Palo Alto, California. If you're ever on the West Coast, drop in and try this classic southern favorite with a twist.

When trying to beat the heat and still enjoy the long days of summer, I hope you get some good ideas for your family from reading and trying some of the Wallace summer favorites.

Andrew at the beach with "short people in pajamas": Caroline, James, and William, 2011

Basted Barbecue Chicken with Carolina-Style Barbecue Sauce

FAMILY FAVORITE • SERVES 6 TO 8

I'm not the biggest fan of "barbecuing" chicken on the grill because it often ends up being overcooked, or even worse, burnt. This is my go-to recipe when I want to bring the outdoor flavors indoors. I especially enjoy the Carolina-style sauce since it is a lighter vinegar-based sauce with a zesty hint of lemon. And when you baste the chicken as it cooks slowly in the oven, it gets a shiny red glaze that is appealing to the eye when serving. This is an easy recipe that I often make ahead and refrigerate and then reheat when ready to serve. (Don't tell anyone, but it's great cold, too!)

FOR THE CAROLINA-STYLE BARBECUE SAUCE

3 large yellow onions, peeled, halved, and cut into ½-inch slices

½ pound (2 sticks) unsalted butter

1 cup apple cider vinegar

1 cup water

⅓ cup sugar

2 tablespoons dry mustard, or 4 tablespoons prepared mustard

1 tablespoon coarse salt

1½ teaspoons freshly ground black pepper

½ teaspoon cayenne pepper

1 large lemon, thinly sliced

2 cups ketchup

⅓ cup Worcestershire sauce

To make the barbecue sauce: In a large, nonstick soup pot, mix the onions, butter, vinegar, water, sugar, mustard, salt, pepper, cayenne, and lemon slices. Over medium-high heat, bring the mixture to a simmer and cook, uncovered, for 20 minutes. Add the ketchup and Worcestershire sauce and bring to a boil. Cook, stirring occasionally, until thickened, about 20 minutes more.

Remove from the heat, let cool, remove the lemon slices from the sauce, and refrigerate until ready to use.

To make the chicken: Rinse the chicken with cold water, and pat dry with paper towels.

Coat a large nonstick roasting pan with nonstick cooking spray and arrange the chicken in a single layer in the pan, being careful not to overcrowd. Generously season the chicken with salt and pepper. Cover with heavy-duty aluminum foil and let stand at room temperature for up to 15 minutes.

Meanwhile, preheat the oven to 300°F.

Place the roasting pan on the center rack of the oven and cook for 1 hour. Remove the foil and drain off the fat and liquid into a measuring cup and reserve for another use.

(recipe continues on page 114)

FOR THE CHICKEN

Two 3- to 3½-pound chickens, each cut into 8 pieces

Nonstick cooking spray

Coarse salt and freshly ground black pepper

2 cups Carolina-Style Barbecue Sauce, plus extra for serving

(continued from page 112)

Using a large spoon, spread half of the sauce and onions over and around the chicken. Cook for another 30 minutes, remove the pan from the oven, spoon over the remaining sauce and onions, and continue to cook for 30 minutes more. Remove from the oven and let rest at room temperature for up to 20 minutes, or until ready to serve. Serve with additional sauce and the pan juices spooned over top.

Sautéed Chicken and Zucchini with Tarragon Pan Sauce

BONELESS, SKINLESS • FAMILY FAVORITE • SERVES 6

I just love growing pots of herbs in our kitchen window. This is a fun recipe that will help you keep your herb containers trimmed and growing more all summer long.

3 pounds boneless, skinless chicken breasts

Coarse salt and freshly ground black pepper

4 tablespoons (½ stick) unsalted butter

2 tablespoons extra-virgin olive oil

4 medium zucchini, cut into ¾-inch pieces

1 cup chicken broth, homemade or store-bought

1 tablespoon chopped fresh tarragon

2 teaspoons freshly squeezed lemon juice

2 tablespoons chopped fresh flat-leaf parsley

Rinse the chicken breasts with cold water and pat dry with paper towels. Season with salt and pepper.

In a large skillet over medium heat, melt 2 tablespoons of the butter and the olive oil. Add the chicken breasts and cook until golden and cooked through, about 6 minutes per side. Transfer to a platter and cover with aluminum foil to keep them warm.

Add the zucchini to the skillet, sprinkle with salt, and cook until crisp-tender, about 2 minutes per side. Using a slotted spoon, transfer the zucchini to a plate lined with paper towels and cover with foil.

Melt the remaining 2 tablespoons butter in the skillet. Add the broth and tarragon and bring to a boil, scraping up the brown bits at the bottom of the skillet. Reduce the heat and simmer until the liquid has reduced by half, 5 to 6 minutes. Remove from the heat and stir in the lemon juice and parsley. Serve the chicken with the sauce and zucchini on a large platter.

Grilled Pesto Chicken

BONELESS, SKINLESS • SERVES 8

Sliced store-bought polenta topped with grilled tomatoes and herbs makes this a delicious one-dish meal.

4 pounds boneless, skinless chicken breasts

Two 7-ounce containers store-bought pesto or homemade (see recipe on page 117)

24 ounces store-bought prepared polenta, sliced 1 inch thick

1 tablespoon extra-virgin olive oil, plus more for brushing

2 pints cherry tomatoes, halved

2 garlic cloves, minced

1 tablespoon chopped fresh basil

Coarse salt and freshly ground black pepper

Rinse the chicken breasts with cold water and pat dry with paper towels. Place the chicken breasts in a resealable plastic bag and pour the pesto over the chicken. Seal the bag and turn it to coat the chicken well. Refrigerate for 4 hours or overnight.

Remove the chicken from the bag and place on a baking sheet, reserving some of the pesto mixture for brushing later. Let the chicken stand for 15 minutes.

Preheat the grill to medium heat (350°F–400°F). Grill the chicken breasts for about 8 minutes on each side, brushing with the reserved pesto when you turn them.

Place the grilled chicken breasts in an ovenproof dish, cover with aluminum foil, and continue to bake in a 300°F oven for an additional 15 minutes.

Brush the polenta slices with a little olive oil. Preheat a grill pan on the stovetop to medium heat. Grill the polenta on each side until crisp and golden brown.

In a medium sauté pan over medium heat, warm 1 tablespoon of the oil. Add the cherry tomatoes and garlic and cook, stirring occasionally, until semisoft, 3 to 5 minutes, depending on the size of the tomatoes. Add the basil and salt and pepper to taste.

Arrange the polenta slices on warm plates, top with 2 tablespoons of the cherry tomato sauce and serve with the chicken.

(recipe continues on page 117)

(continued from page 115)

2 cloves garlic

2 cups fresh basil leaves, firmly packed

½ cup freshly grated Parmesan cheese

⅓ cup pine nuts

1 teaspoon coarse salt

½ cup extra-virgin olive oil

PESTO

In a food processor fitted with the steel blade, add the garlic and pulse several times until minced. Add the basil leaves and pulse again several times. Add the cheese, nuts, and salt and pulse until well chopped. As the food processor is running, drizzle the olive oil through the feed tube until the pesto is well combined.

Creamy Chicken Salad

BONELESS, SKINLESS • SERVES 8 TO 10

The eggs add moisture to this recipe and allow you to control the amount of mayonnaise to create that "old-fashioned" picnic flavor, creamy and rich.

1 quart water

4 boneless, skinless chicken breasts

1 tablespoon extra-virgin olive oil

1 teaspoon whole black peppercorns

½ teaspoon coarse salt

1 bay leaf

4 stalks celery, cut into ¾-inch dice

1½ cups mayonnaise, or less if desired

1 teaspoon celery salt

3 hard-boiled large eggs

Coarse salt and freshly ground black pepper

Place a large skillet with a tight-fitting lid over medium-high heat and add the water, chicken breasts, oil, peppercorns, salt, and bay leaf. Bring to a simmer, then immediately remove the skillet from the heat. Cover and let stand until the chicken is tender, about 12 minutes.

Transfer the chicken breasts to a plate and let cool.

Place the celery in a large bowl. Shred the cooled chicken with your fingers or with a fork and add to the celery in the bowl. Add the mayonnaise, celery salt, and salt and pepper to taste and toss until evenly coated. Crush the hard-boiled eggs with your hands and fold into the salad. Chill the salad and serve in a large bowl.

Herbed Buttermilk "Not-Fried" Chicken

From the kitchen of Vana Martin

FAMILY FAVORITE • SERVES 6

Cornflake-crusted chicken is one of the first recipes I remember my mom preparing from my childhood. I have fond memories of enjoying this chicken on boat rides down the Potomac River on lazy summer afternoons and early evenings. I make a lot of this baked "not-fried" chicken to enjoy cold all the time. I've changed my mother's recipe a bit and soak the chicken in an herbed buttermilk bath to make it more flavorful.

Two 3½-pound chickens,
    each cut into 8 pieces

4 cups buttermilk

4 garlic cloves, crushed

2 teaspoons dried rosemary

2 teaspoons dried marjoram

2 teaspoons dried sage

2 teaspoons dried thyme

1½ teaspoons coarse salt

1 teaspoon cayenne pepper

Nonstick cooking spray

8 cups cornflakes cereal, crushed

Coarse salt and freshly ground
    black pepper

8 tablespoons (1 stick) unsalted
    butter, melted

Rinse the chicken pieces with cold water and pat dry with paper towels.

In a large bowl, stir together the buttermilk, garlic, rosemary, marjoram, sage, thyme, salt, and cayenne. Add the chicken and turn to coat well. Cover and refrigerate for 4 hours or overnight.

Preheat the oven to 350°F. Line 2 baking sheets with aluminum foil and then coat with nonstick cooking spray.

Remove the chicken from the refrigerator and let stand at room temperature for 15 minutes.

Place the crushed cornflakes in a shallow dish and sprinkle with a pinch of salt and pepper. Roll the chicken pieces in the cornflakes to coat and set on the prepared baking sheets. Bake the chicken for 15 minutes, then switch the baking sheets and rotate onto alternate racks and brush and drizzle with the melted butter. Continue to cook for 45 minutes more.

Oven-Grilled Chicken with Roasted Grape Tomatoes

GOOD FOR COMPANY • SERVES 6 TO 8

Roasted red tomatoes combined with savory capers and fresh parsley make for a wonderful topping on this oven-grilled chicken.

FOR THE CHICKEN

6 tablespoons freshly squeezed lemon juice

3 tablespoons grated lemon zest

6 garlic cloves, minced

3 large whole chicken breasts, 4 chicken leg portions (thighs and drumsticks, attached)

1½ teaspoons coarse salt

¾ teaspoon freshly ground black pepper

FOR THE TOMATOES

4 cups grape tomatoes

2 tablespoons extra-virgin olive oil

1 tablespoon finely grated lemon zest

2 garlic cloves, minced

2 tablespoons chopped fresh flat-leaf parsley

3 tablespoons capers

Coarse salt and freshly ground black pepper

Nonstick cooking spray

To prepare the chicken: Place the lemon juice, zest, and minced garlic in a large resealable plastic bag. Add the chicken to the bag and refrigerate for 4 hours. Remove the chicken and set aside for 15 minutes. Remove the garlic bits from the chicken and lightly season with the salt and pepper.

To prepare the tomatoes: While the chicken is marinating, preheat the oven to 425°F. Combine the tomatoes, olive oil, lemon zest, and garlic on a baking sheet and toss gently. Bake for 15 minutes, or until the tomatoes are tender. Combine the tomato mixture with the parsley and capers and season with salt and pepper.

Preheat the grill to medium-high heat (450°F–500°F). Reduce the oven temperature to 350°F. Coat a baking sheet with nonstick cooking spray.

Place the chicken on the grill rack and cook for 5 minutes per side to make grill marks.

Transfer the chicken to the prepared baking sheet and bake in the oven for 20 minutes. Serve the chicken and tomatoes on a large platter.

Stovetop Summer Chicken

STOVETOP • SERVES 4

This stovetop dish is a wonderful way to beat the heat and still enjoy a crispy golden chicken without all the mess of frying. It reminds me of a great Tuscan roasted chicken. I just love the flavor of cooking in a cast-iron skillet.

One 3-pound chicken, backbone removed, butterflied (see What is Butterflying? on page 25)

6 tablespoons extra-virgin olive oil, plus additional to rub chicken

3 garlic cloves, minced

2 tablespoons chopped fresh rosemary

1 tablespoon chopped fresh thyme

Coarse salt and freshly ground black pepper

Remove the chicken from the refrigerator, rinse with cold water, and pat dry with paper towels. Rub olive oil on the chicken to coat. Let stand for 15 minutes.

In a cast-iron skillet over medium heat, warm the 6 tablespoons of oil. Place the chicken in the skillet, breast side down, reduce the heat to medium-low, and cook for 15 to 18 minutes. Using tongs, turn the chicken over, breast side up, and cover with the garlic and herbs.

Cook for 20 minutes more, basting occasionally with the oil and juices in the pan.

Transfer the chicken to a cutting board and sprinkle with salt and pepper to taste. Cover with aluminum foil, let rest for 10 minutes, then carve and serve.

Skewers of Sage Chicken with Sweet Italian Sausage

FAMILY FAVORITE • GRILL • SERVES 6

This is one of my Father's Day favorites to serve to honor Chris! The rustic sausage and savory sage makes this a meat lover's meal. Think of this dish as a night out at a Brazilian steak house.

FOR THE ROSEMARY-GARLIC OIL

1½ cups extra-virgin olive oil

6 garlic cloves, smashed and peeled

2 sprigs fresh rosemary, chopped

FOR THE SKEWERS

2 pounds boneless, skinless chicken thighs, trimmed of excess fat and cut in half

½ cup plus 2 tablespoons Rosemary-Garlic Oil

1 tablespoon chopped fresh rosemary

Coarse salt and freshly ground black pepper

2 pounds sweet Italian sausages, cut into 2-inch pieces

24 large fresh sage leaves

Six 12-inch metal skewers

To make the rosemary-garlic oil: Combine all the ingredients in a small bowl and whisk well. Set aside.

Up to a day ahead or 4 hours prior to cooking, rinse the chicken thighs in cold water and pat dry with paper towels. Toss the chicken with 2 tablespoons of the rosemary-garlic oil and the chopped rosemary. Season with salt and pepper. Cover and refrigerate.

Preheat the grill to medium-high heat (350°F–450°F). Place the ½ cup of rosemary-garlic oil in a small dish for brushing the skewers while grilling. Thread 3 pieces of the sausage, chicken, and sage leaves alternately on the metal skewers. Grill the skewers, covered, until one side is browned and has nice grill marks, about 4 minutes. Brush with the rosemary-garlic oil, flip, and cook until the other side is cooked, about 4 minutes more.

Continue to cook, turning and brushing with the oil, until the sausage and chicken are both cooked through, about 10 minutes more. Cover with aluminum foil and let rest for a couple of minutes. To serve, arrange the skewers on a large platter and drizzle with the remaining rosemary-garlic oil.

Note: *The fragrant rosemary-garlic oil is also delicious as a dipping oil for Italian bread. Or try rubbing it on slices of bread prior to grilling.*

Butterflied Grilled Chicken with Ginger-Citrus Marinade

$ • GRILL • SERVES 4

The citrus-ginger marinade makes this a zesty chicken dish to prepare on the grill. Since it is light in calories, I like to serve it with my corn pudding that marries together all the sweet tastes of summer.

¾ cup canola oil

¾ cup freshly squeezed orange juice

3 small lemons, thinly sliced

3 scallions, white and green parts, thinly sliced

6 tablespoons honey

One 3-inch piece fresh ginger, peeled and thinly sliced

Finely grated zest of 2 limes

¾ teaspoon coarse salt

¾ teaspoon freshly ground black pepper

One 3-pound chicken, backbone removed, butterflied (see What is Butterflying? on page 25)

In a large bowl, combine the oil, orange juice, lemon slices, scallions, honey, ginger, lime zest, salt, and pepper. Add the chicken and coat it with the marinade. Marinate, refrigerated, turning occasionally, for 4 hours or overnight.

Remove the chicken from the refrigerator 15 minutes prior to grilling, turning the chicken over in the marinade one more time.

Preheat a grill to medium-high heat (450°F–500°F).

Remove the chicken from the marinade and reserve the marinade for basting. Place the chicken on the grill, breast side down, and cook for 5 minutes on each side to make grill marks. If cooking on a gas grill, turn off the middle burners and place the chicken in the middle. If using a charcoal grill, move the coals to one side and place the chicken on the side of the grill without any coals. Baste the chicken with the marinade, cover with a piece of aluminum foil, and press this down with a heavy oven-proof plate. Cook, covered, for about 20 minutes, then turn over and brush with more of the marinade, and continue to cook for 20 minutes more, until cooked through.

Transfer the chicken to a cutting board. Cover with foil and let rest for at least 10 minutes. Grill the lemon slices until they have grill marks. Cut the chicken into 4 pieces and transfer to a serving platter, then garnish with the grilled lemon slices.

Grilled Chicken and Herbed Farfalle Pasta Salad

BONELESS, SKINLESS • FAMILY FAVORITE • GRILL • SERVES 6 TO 8

Talk about fresh—this family favorite is full of light tastes with all of the herbs that are gently tossed with the pasta and chicken. Leaving the herbs in large pieces adds a refreshing rustic quality to this pasta salad.

1 pound box farfalle (bow tie) pasta

½ cup plus 2 tablespoons extra-virgin olive oil

4 boneless, skinless chicken breasts (about 8 ounces each)

Coarse salt and freshly ground black pepper

7 tablespoons freshly squeezed lemon juice

3 garlic cloves, minced

1 teaspoon ground cumin

1 cup fresh cilantro sprigs

¼ cup fresh hand-torn flat-leaf parsley leaves

¼ cup hand-torn fresh basil leaves

¼ cup hand-torn fresh mint leaves

1½ cups fresh arugula, tough stems removed

¾ cup crumbled feta cheese

Lemon wedges, for serving

In a large pot of boiling salted water, cook the farfalle until al dente according to the package directions, 10 to 12 minutes. Drain the pasta and immediately toss with 1 tablespoon of the olive oil. Let the pasta cool completely in the refrigerator.

Preheat a grill to medium-high heat (350°F–400°F). Rinse the chicken with cold water, and pat dry with paper towels.

Brush the chicken with a tablespoon of the oil and grill the breasts until golden on each side, 4 to 5 minutes. Season with salt and pepper. Let the chicken cool, then cut it on the diagonal into thin strips, and set aside.

In a large bowl whisk the remaining ½ cup of oil with the lemon juice, garlic, and cumin. Season to taste with salt and pepper. Add the farfalle, chicken, cilantro, parsley, basil, and mint to the bowl and combine. Add the arugula and season to taste with additional salt and pepper, if needed. Toss in the feta cheese. Transfer the salad to a large pasta bowl and garnish with lemon wedges.

Grilled Chicken Paillards

BONELESS, SKINLESS • QUICK • GRILL • SERVES 4

When the farm stands and markets are abundant with fresh lettuces, I like to prepare these simple paillards and serve them hot from the grill, topped with a fresh lettuce salad tossed with lemon juice and olive oil.

4 boneless, skinless chicken breasts (6 to 8 ounces each), trimmed

Coarse salt and freshly ground pepper

Crushed red pepper flakes

2 garlic cloves, minced

2 tablespoons chopped fresh rosemary, chopped

¼ cup freshly squeezed lemon juice

¼ cup extra-virgin olive oil, plus more for drizzling

4 lemon wedges, for serving

Rinse the chicken with cold water and pat dry with paper towels. Place each chicken breast on a sheet of plastic wrap. Place another sheet of plastic wrap on top, and, using the flat side of a meat mallet, pound out to form thin paillards with a thickness of about ¼ inch. Pound out the remaining chicken breasts to form paillards and place them on an aluminum foil–lined baking sheet. Generously season each paillard on both sides with salt, pepper, and red pepper flakes. Sprinkle both sides with the garlic and rosemary. Drizzle both sides with the lemon juice and ¼ cup of the olive oil.

Preheat a grill to high heat (500°F–600°F).

Arrange the paillards on the grill and cook until firm to the touch, 1 to 2 minutes per side, using a long wide spatula to move and turn the paillards. Transfer the paillards to a serving platter, drizzle with olive oil and garnish with the lemon wedges.

Chicken Kebabs with Creamy Pesto Sauce

BONELESS, SKINLESS • FAMILY FAVORITE • SERVES 8

Here is a great recipe that you can prepare in less than 15 minutes using the broiler, and makes a colorful presentation no matter when you choose to serve it.

2 pounds boneless, skinless chicken breasts

Nonstick cooking spray

8 teaspoons freshly squeezed lemon juice

4 teaspoons finely grated lemon zest

4 teaspoons minced garlic

4 teaspoons extra-virgin olive oil

1 teaspoon coarse salt

½ teaspoon freshly ground black pepper

1 yellow bell pepper, cut into 16 pieces

16 cherry tomatoes

1 medium red onion, cut into 16 wedges

Eight 12-inch skewers

¼ cup plain yogurt

¼ cup sour cream

2 tablespoons store-bought pesto, or more to taste

Rinse the chicken in cold water and pat dry with paper towels. Cut into 1-inch pieces. Set aside.

Preheat the broiler to high heat. Coat a baking sheet with nonstick cooking spray.

In a large bowl, combine 6 teaspoons of the lemon juice, zest, garlic, oil, salt, and pepper. Toss in the chicken, bell pepper pieces, cherry tomatoes, and onion wedges. Thread the vegetables and chicken onto eight 12-inch skewers and place on the prepared baking sheet. Broil the kebabs for 6 minutes on one side, then turn and cook on the opposite side for 6 minutes, or until the chicken is cooked through and the vegetables have started to brown.

In a small bowl, combine the remaining 2 teaspoons of lemon juice, the yogurt, sour cream, and pesto. Serve the sauce with the kebabs on a large platter.

Tip: If using bamboo skewers, they must be soaked in water for at least 30 minutes to prevent burning. Then drain them and thread the food to be grilled onto the skewers, covering as much area on the skewer as possible.

Southern Oven "Unfried" Chicken

From the kitchen of Chef Art Smith

BONELESS, SKINLESS • SERVES 4

This is Chef Art Smith's signature dish at his Palo Alto, California, Lyfe Kitchen restaurant. It is his healthier take on a classic Southern favorite.

4 boneless, skinless chicken breasts

1 cup buttermilk

1 tablespoon Louisiana hot sauce

1½ cups whole-wheat panko bread crumbs

3 tablespoons freshly grated Parmesan cheese

2 teaspoons freshly ground black pepper

2 teaspoons crushed red pepper flakes

1½ teaspoons onion powder

1½ teaspoons garlic powder

1 teaspoon paprika

Butter-flavored spray oil

Preheat the oven to 400°F.

Rinse the chicken in cold water and pat dry with paper towels. In a large bowl, combine the buttermilk and hot sauce. Submerge the chicken breasts in the buttermilk marinade. Allow to soak at least 1 hour or in the refrigerator for up to 24 hours.

While the chicken is marinating, fill a large plastic bag with the panko bread crumbs, Parmesan, pepper, red pepper flakes, onion powder, garlic powder, and paprika. Shake to blend. Using tongs, remove the chicken breasts from the marinade and place them directly into the bag of bread crumbs and spices. Discard the marinade. Close the bag and shake well, until the chicken breasts are evenly coated with bread crumbs. Remove the breaded chicken breasts from the bag and lay flat on a lightly oiled sheet pan. Discard the bag with any remaining bread crumbs and spices. Allow to chill, uncovered, in the refrigerator for 30 minutes.

Lightly coat each chicken breast with the butter-flavored spray oil and bake for 35 to 40 minutes.

Friends and Family

In this chapter, I want to share different recipes I have gathered from our dear family and friends at memorable times gathered around their tables.

Godparents are special members of our extended family. They have always been at my side, as my children have grown up. Sarah's godmother, Diana Muss, was my best riding buddy in Virginia hunt country. We not only rode together, but also raised our children together before I met Chris. We always went out to Diana and her husband Josh's farm for the last lunch of the summer. We were headed there on Labor Day, 2001 when Diana passed away tragically in a riding accident. In this chapter, Josh shares with us Diana's classic Chicken Divan, which is tasty and creamy served over a bed of jasmine rice. Remick's godmother, Patty Warrender, is another old friend from the country. When she is not busy raising Norwich terriers, she is a fantastic cook. Patty's Roasted Chicken is a recipe that she found years ago, but continues to make weekly!

Bonnie McElveen-Hunter is such a supportive friend. When I told her I wanted to write a soup cookbook, she said you can do it! And I did with her support and encouragement. Bonnie is the founder and CEO of Pace Communications in North Carolina. Pace publishes many of the magazines you see on airplanes or in your hotel room. She was the first woman to serve as Chairman of the Board of Governors of the American Red Cross and during her tenure, she oversaw relief efforts after Hurricane Katrina. Bonnie has so much energy and keeps her trim figure by eating the Curry Chicken Salad she contributed to this book. It contains no mayonnaise, and the curry and golden raisins add a lot of flavor. It's a dish I often crave. It's very easy to make and great to have on hand in the refrigerator for lunch, or just to snack on by the forkful whenever you're hungry.

My neighbor and friend Ann Free shared with me a favorite recipe that she enjoyed, growing up in the South, at lunches or festive dinner parties. Her Hot Chicken Salad Pie calls for a simple Ritz cracker crust, a filling of poached chicken combined with onion and celery, a slivered almond topping, and bakes in the oven in under an hour. This recipe is a nice alternative to quiche. Ann loves to entertain and I have learned so much from her sense of style and taste. She is also the reason we

have our beloved Labrador, Winston. I dropped over to see her around Valentine's Day almost a decade ago, and there I met Beryl, who was a six-week-old adorable yellow Labrador puppy. I begged and begged to get a puppy, too. And finally on my birthday that year, Chris surprised me with Beryl's half-brother, chubby little Winston who came from the same breeder.

A more recent addition to our neighborhood, but also a dear friend, is Angela Newnam. We try to get our neighbors together for potluck dinners every season, just to catch up with everyone's lives. Angela runs a company that sells lovely panties, called Knock-Out! She and her daughter Anna created Chicken Tacos with a secret guacamole.

Like so many parents, we have met some of our best friends through our children. When Sarah and Remick started school in Potomac, Maryland, I organized a carpool to take them and several other kids from our neighborhood in the city out to school each morning. That is how I met Robin Jeffery. Robin introduced me to a wonderful Mediterranean Chicken, a recipe that she adapted from the *The Silver Palate Cookbook*. She uses boneless chicken because her family won't eat anything on a bone. She adds pitted prunes and Spanish olives and marinates it overnight, which produces a savory sauce when baked.

top: Ann Hand working and designing jewelry at her shop. *above:* Anna and Angela Newnam at home, Fall 2011

The Caseys are other friends we met when our daughter Sarah was in high school with the Casey girls. Sharon makes a delicious Asian Chicken Salad.

I go way back with Laurie and Bob Monahan, who now have three lovely daughters. They introduced Chris and me to Round Hill, a classic resort just outside of Montego Bay in Jamaica. When visiting their home, I learned to make their family recipe for Jerk Chicken, brought home from their travels to Jamaica and inspired by the love of the traditions of the island.

Ann Hand is the founder and owner of a distinctive jewelry store in Washington. She designed the famous Liberty Eagle pin that First Ladies Hillary Clinton and Laura Bush both wore on many occasions. Her husband, Lloyd, is one of Washington's top lawyers. And back in the '60s, he served as President Lyndon Johnson's Chief of Protocol. Ann shares her Texas Fried Chicken recipe that she likes to serve with creamy mashed potatoes and pecan pie. Calories don't count when food is this good!

above: Meredith, Sharon, and Christine Casey at home.
below: Diana Muss and me, Opening Day Orange County Hunt.
Photo by Mary Phillips Coker.

top: The Jeffery family on safari: Jocelynn, Ben, Robin, Reuben, and Bob. *center:* The Monahan family: Kate, Laurie, Bob, Brooke, and Kelly. *bottom:* Dick Dubin with Chris, Palm Beach, 2011

Years ago, my friend Liz Dubin wrote a cookbook with members of her community called *A Tasteful Collection* to raise money for the Hebrew Home women's auxiliary. I was thrilled when Liz had me to her home for lunch and gave me a signed copy of the book. As we were looking through the recipes, I noticed the classic Chicken Kiev and how decadent it was, prepared with so much herbed butter and then fried. We decided to re-create this classic dish by baking it and substituting a panko crust to lower the fat content. It is just as good as the original, and it still pops when you pierce it with a fork!

Last, but not least, in "Friends and Family," you'll find recipes from my mother, from Chris's sister Pauline, and from our son Peter. My mom, Vana Martin (aka "Nana"), cooks for me when I go to visit her. "No Peek" Chicken is just that—chicken and rice combined with soup that you cover tightly with aluminum foil and bake. It is so good I like to eat it cold the next day! Pauline makes an Easy Roast Chicken that is prepared with just lemon and salt, which her mother used to

make for her as a child when they lived in Haiti. Simple but delicious! Our son Peter spends the summer with his young family in Bridgehampton, outside of New York City. He loves to grill, and introduced us to a delicious dinner he and his wonderful wife Jennifer like to make. Believe it or not, Peter is brave enough to make Beer Can Chicken, a recipe in which he places a half empty can of Budweiser (drinking the other half of the beer is part of the

top. Ann Free with Winston's half brother Beryl.
above: Patty Warrender with her Norwich terriers, Summer 2011

fun) in the cavity of the chicken and then cooks it on the grill over indirect heat for the moistest chicken ever. This recipe is perfect because we get to spend time playing with our grandchildren, William, Caroline, and James, while Peter is the grill master.

This introduction to "Friends and Family" is long, but we treasure all of the people who gave me the recipes for their special dishes. Thank you for being in our lives and for the joy you bring us every day.

Ann's Hot Chicken Salad Pie

From the kitchen of Ann Free

GOOD FOR COMPANY • MAKES 2 PIES; ABOUT 12 SERVINGS

This is a wonderful recipe to serve for an elegant lunch or Sunday supper with friends. Ann entertains often because her husband Jim is a very active businessman. Her buffets are scrumptious and this dish is just one small example of her enormous creativity.

3 boneless, skinless, chicken breasts (about 1 pound)

1 quart water

1 tablespoon extra-virgin olive oil

½ teaspoon coarse salt

70 Ritz crackers

8 tablespoons (1 stick) unsalted butter, melted

2 cups cooked rice

1 medium onion, diced

½ cup chopped celery

½ teaspoon cayenne pepper

One 10¾-ounce can cream of mushroom soup

1 cup mayonnaise

4 hard-boiled large eggs, finely chopped

4 teaspoons freshly squeezed lemon juice (about ½ lemon)

Pinch of coarse salt

1 cup slivered almonds

Preheat the oven to 350°F.

Rinse the chicken breasts with cold water and pat dry with paper towels.

Set a large skillet with a tight-fitting lid over medium-high heat and add the water, oil, and salt, then add the chicken breasts. Bring to a simmer, then immediately remove the skillet from the heat. Cover and let stand until the chicken is tender, about 12 minutes. Using tongs or a slotted spoon, lift the chicken breasts from the water and transfer to a plate to cool. When cool, shred the chicken, place it in a large bowl, and set aside.

Make the first crust: Place 35 of the crackers into a large resealable plastic bag and crush finely with a meat mallet or a rolling pin. Pour the crumbs into a mixing bowl and add 4 tablespoons of the melted butter. Mix to combine. Press the mixture into a 9-inch glass pie plate with your hands, making sure to firmly press the crumbs onto the bottom and the sides of the pie plate. Repeat the procedure, using the remaining crackers and melted butter, to make the second crust and press into a second 9-inch glass pie plate.

Bake the crusts for 10 minutes.

Meanwhile, make the pie filling: Add the cooked rice, onion, celery, cayenne, mushroom soup, mayonnaise, hard-boiled eggs, lemon juice, and a pinch of salt to the bowl with the shredded chicken. Fold all the ingredients together until well combined.

  (recipe continues on page 138)

(continued from page 136)

Carefully fill each of the pie shells with half of the filling mixture, making sure not to disturb the cracker crusts. Bake the pies for 35 to 40 minutes.

While the pies are baking, toast the almonds in a small skillet over high heat, stirring frequently, until the nuts begin to brown, 3 to 5 minutes.

When the pies are almost baked, sprinkle half of the nuts onto the top of each pie and continue to bake for another 5 minutes. Remove the pies from the oven and allow to rest at room temperature for at least 20 minutes before serving.

Newnam's Chicken Tacos with Anna's Secret Guacamole

From the kitchen of Angela and Anna Newnam

BONELESS, SKINLESS • QUICK • SERVES 6

The Newnam family is always on the go! This is their tried-and-true healthy recipe that brings them together at the end of a jam-packed day. The best part of this dish is that the children often help prepare the dish and once it is done, it is self-serve!

FOR THE SECRET GUACAMOLE

6 medium to soft avocados, coarsely chopped

2 medium tomatoes, finely chopped

½ Vidalia onion, finely chopped

½ cup cilantro, stems removed and finely chopped

Juice of 2 limes (about 4 tablespoons)

½ teaspoon freshly ground black pepper

Coarse salt

To prepare the guacamole: Slice the avocados in half lengthwise, remove the seeds, and, using a spoon, scoop out the flesh from each. Place in a bowl and coarsely chop. Save 3 of the seeds to return to the bowl to keep the guacamole from browning until ready to serve. Add the tomatoes, onion, cilantro, lime juice, pepper, and salt to the avocados and mix with a fork until you reach the desired consistency. Return the seeds to the guacamole and mix in, cover with plastic wrap, and refrigerate for up to 3 days.

FOR THE TACOS

2½ pounds free-range boneless, skinless chicken breasts

2 tablespoons canola oil

1 teaspoon coarse salt

1 teaspoon whole coriander seeds

1 bay leaf

2 slices lime

1 large Vidalia onion, chopped

1 cup canned chopped tomatoes, drained

2 medium red bell peppers, seeded and chopped

1 medium yellow bell pepper, seeded and chopped

½ cup fresh cilantro leaves

One 4-ounce can chopped green chilies and their liquid

1 teaspoon ancho chili powder

½ teaspoon crushed red pepper flakes

1 tablespoon freshly squeezed lime juice

Coarse salt and freshly ground black pepper

12 soft- or hard-shell tacos, warmed

1½ cups shredded cheddar cheese

1 cup plain yogurt or sour cream

Anna's Secret Guacamole, or store-bought

Your favorite store-bought salsa

1 head iceberg lettuce, shredded

To prepare the tacos: Rinse the chicken with cold water and pat dry with paper towels. Place a large skillet with a tight-fitting lid over medium-high heat and add enough water to cover the chicken breasts (about 8 cups). Add the chicken, ½ teaspoon of the oil, salt, coriander seeds, bay leaf, and lime slices. Bring to a simmer, then immediately remove the skillet from the heat. Cover and let stand until the chicken is tender, about 12 minutes. Using tongs or a slotted spoon, lift the chicken breasts from the broth and transfer to a plate to cool. Reserve ½ cup of the broth and strain through a fine-mesh sieve. When the chicken is cool, cut it into ¾-inch chunks.

In a large heavy-duty skillet over medium-high heat, warm the remaining canola oil and the strained, reserved ½ cup broth. Add the onion, tomatoes, bell peppers, cilantro, and green chilies with their liquid and bring to a simmer. Cook until softened, 4 to 6 minutes.

Return the chicken to the skillet and add the ancho chili powder and red pepper flakes along with the lime juice. Stir to combine and continue to simmer until heated throughout. Taste and adjust the seasoning with salt and pepper, if needed. Serve with warm tacos, cheese, sour cream, guacamole, salsa, and shredded lettuce in bowls on the table.

Monahan Family's Jerk Chicken

From the kitchen of the Monahan family, by Ann Gray

FAMILY FAVORITE • SERVES 4 TO 6

Ann is the award-winning chef for our dear friends, the Monahans, and their large family. Laurie invited me over to cook with Ann on an early June day and we made her Jerk Chicken. This is a twist on Jerk Chicken because it is baked whole, but believe me, it uses all the spices known in Jamaican cooking and is so good. Their daughter Brooke, who is a vegetarian, says, "This is the first dish I would eat if I were not a vegetarian." This is her husband Bob's favorite recipe, which he eats twice a week.

One 4½- to 5-pound chicken

1 tablespoon coarse salt

2 shallots, peeled and left whole

1 large yellow onion, halved lengthwise and sliced into half-moons

3 celery stalks, cut into ¼-inch pieces

6 garlic cloves, peeled and left whole

One 10-ounce jar of premade Jerk sauce, like Walkersville (available on the Internet)

6 small white potatoes, peeled (optional)

Rinse the chicken inside and out with cold water and pat dry with paper towels. Season the chicken inside and out with the salt.

Position a rack in the center of the oven. Preheat the oven to 450°F.

Place the shallots and some of the onion and celery inside the cavity. Place the garlic and the rest of the vegetables in the bottom of an ovenproof dish large enough to hold the chicken. Rub 2 tablespoons of the jerk sauce all over the entire chicken. Place the chicken on top of the vegetables in the dish and cover tightly with aluminum foil. Let stand at room temperature for 15 minutes until ready to bake. Remove the foil and bake the chicken for 1 hour. If using the optional small white potatoes, add them at this point to the vegetables in the bottom of the dish. Add ½ cup of water and baste the chicken with the pan juices. Spread the thighs out with a fork, baste again, and continue cooking until the thigh juices run clear and the potatoes are soft, about ½ hour more.

Remove from oven and let rest for approximately 10 minutes before serving.

Bonnie's Curry Chicken Salad

From the kitchen of Bonnie McElveen-Hunter

BONELESS, SKINLESS • POTLUCK • SERVES 8 TO 12

Bonnie is always on the go, doing so many wonderful things for organizations and helping friends. This is her secret recipe to stay focused and fueled for her high-energy life.

3 whole boneless, skinless chicken breasts, split in half (about 3 pounds)

Coarse salt and freshly ground black pepper

1 quart water

1 teaspoon extra-virgin olive oil

12 ounces Greek-style yogurt or plain yogurt (about 1½ cups)

1 cup golden raisins

1 cup chopped walnuts

½ cup finely chopped celery

2 teaspoons curry powder

Toasted sprouted rye or wheat bread, or raisin bread, for serving

Honey mustard (optional), for spreading

Rinse the chicken breasts with cold water and pat dry with paper towels. Season with salt and pepper.

Place a large skillet with a tight-fitting lid over medium-high heat and add the water, oil, and ½ teaspoon salt. Add the chicken breasts, bring to a simmer, then immediately remove the skillet from the heat. Cover and let stand until tender, about 12 minutes. Using tongs or a slotted spoon, transfer the chicken to a plate to cool.

Combine the yogurt, raisins, walnuts, celery, curry powder, 1 teaspoon salt, and ½ teaspoon pepper and blend well. Shred the chicken with a fork or your fingers and add to the yogurt mixture, tossing to coat thoroughly. Serve the chicken salad on toasted sprouted rye or wheat bread, or toasted raisin bread. And for an extra kick, spread the bread first with honey mustard, if desired.

> Note: *To plump up the raisins and create a moister sandwich, soak the raisins in a cup of warm water for 15 minutes. Drain and squeeze with some paper towels before using in the recipe.*

Peter's Beer Can Chicken

From the kitchen of Peter Wallace

FAMILY FAVORITE • GRILL • SERVES 4 TO 6

Chris's eldest son, Peter Wallace, thinks nothing of firing up his grill to make this moist chicken. The beer and herbs make for a perfect casual afternoon lunch or evening dinner because once it is on the grill you can kick back and relax with your family and friends. For an additional layer of flavor, add 4 handfuls of hickory wood chips, soaked in water for 30 minutes and then drained, right to the top of the smoker box of a gas grill. When the chips begin to smoke, transfer the bird to the grill using a beer can rack, which allows the chicken to stand securely upright. You can find the beer can stand on the Internet or at most kitchen stores.

One 4-pound chicken

¼ cup coarse salt

2 teaspoons onion powder

2 teaspoons garlic powder

1 teaspoon chili powder

½ teaspoon freshly ground
  black pepper

One 12-ounce can Budweiser,
  at room temperature

Remove and discard the neck, giblets, and excess fat from the chicken. Rinse the chicken inside and out with cold water and pat dry with paper towels. Generously sprinkle the salt over the entire surface and inside the cavity. Cover the chicken with plastic wrap and let stand at room temperature for 15 minutes.

Prepare a gas grill for indirect cooking over low heat (300°F–350°F), and cover until the grill reaches 325°F.

In a small bowl, mix together the onion powder, garlic powder, chili powder, and pepper.

Season the chicken all over with the rub, including inside the cavity and a little under the skin. Fold the wing tips behind the chicken's back.

Open the beer can and pour off half the beer—or drink it! Using a can opener, make two more holes on the top of the can. Place the beer can in the beer can rack and plunk the chicken over the beer can. Transfer the rack with the chicken to the grill and grill over indirect medium heat with the lid closed, until the juices run clear, about 1 hour and 15 minutes. An instant-read thermometer should read 165°F when inserted into the thickest part of the breast.

Gently remove the chicken from the grill with large tongs and place on a casserole dish you place under the can stand. Let it rest for 10 minutes, then remove the can of beer from the cavity with oven mitts and large tongs. Carve the chicken into pieces and serve on a large platter.

Nana's "No Peek" Chicken

From the kitchen of Vana Martin

ONE POT • $ • SERVES 4

When I go to visit my mom in Florida, this is the dish I most often request on the first day I arrive. I like to take her out to lunch when I visit, but we have so much to talk about on our first day together that our jaws hurt when we go to bed at night. This is her easy, "No Peek" chicken, which she makes so we don't miss any talking time.

4 to 6 bone-in, skinless chicken thighs

One 6.9-ounce box chicken-flavored Rice-A-Roni

1 can cream of mushroom soup

One 10¼-ounce can cream of celery soup

1 cup cold water

1 teaspoon dried parsley

1 package dried onion soup

Rinse the chicken with cold water and pat dry with paper towels. Preheat the oven to 350°F. Lightly grease a 13 × 9-inch casserole dish.

In a bowl, mix together the Rice-A-Roni, canned soups, water, and parsley, then spread out the mixture in the prepared casserole dish. Place the chicken pieces on top and sprinkle with the dried onion soup mix. Seal the casserole with aluminum foil and bake for 2½ hours—no peeking!

Sharon's Asian Chicken Salad

From the kitchen of Sharon Casey

BONELESS, SKINLESS • QUICK • SERVES 8 GENEROUSLY

Sharon "sneakily" got this recipe from the chef at an Atlanta restaurant during college tours with her daughter Meredith. Sharon said she had food allergies and needed to know the ingredients for the salad. This favorite recipe is often served at the Casey house when we girls get together for lunch.

2 pounds boneless, skinless chicken breasts

1 quart water

1 tablespoon sesame oil

One 1-inch piece fresh ginger, peeled and sliced into 6 pieces

½ teaspoon coarse salt

1 cup unseasoned rice wine vinegar

¼ cup hot Chinese mustard

¼ cup mayonnaise

1 tablespoon sugar

3 tablespoons soy sauce

Juice of 1 medium lime

One 16-ounce bag shredded cabbage mix (about 5 cups)

One 8-ounce bag shredded red cabbage (about 2½ cups)

1 cup chopped fresh cilantro

1 cup fried Chinese chow mein noodles

Toasted sesame seeds (optional)

Rinse the chicken with cold water and pat dry with paper towels. Place a large skillet with a tight-fitting lid over medium-high heat and add the water, sesame oil, ginger, and salt. Add the chicken breasts, bring to a simmer, then immediately remove the pan from the heat. Cover and let stand until tender, about 12 minutes.

Meanwhile, make the dressing. In a small bowl, whisk together the vinegar, mustard, mayonnaise, sugar, soy sauce, and lime juice until combined.

Place the shredded cabbages in a large serving bowl. When the chicken is cool enough to handle, shred the chicken, using a fork or your fingers. Add the shredded chicken to the cabbage mixture and top with the chopped cilantro. Add the dressing and toss well to combine. When ready to serve, garnish with the chow mein noodles and sesame seeds, if using.

> Helpful Hint: *The salad can be made a day ahead but the dressing should not be combined with the cabbage and chicken mixture sooner than an hour before serving since the vinegar often leaches the color from the red cabbage, which can turn the salad pink, and the noodles can become soggy.*

Ann's Texas Fried Chicken

From the kitchen of Ann Hand

FEED A CROWD • SERVES 6 TO 8

Ann Hand is the sweetest friend, and the savvy founder and owner of Ann Hand, LLC, one of the most distinctive and prominent jewelry design firms in Washington, D.C. She has a huge heart and is very involved with the Armed Services, the United States Naval Academy, the United States Military Academy at West Point, and the U.S. House of Representatives, where she designs brooches for the spouses. Here she brings us a favorite recipe from her Texas roots.

Two 3½-pound broiler-fryer chickens, cut into 6 pieces

⅔ cup evaporated milk

1 large egg, beaten

1¼ cups all-purpose flour

1 teaspoon coarse salt

1 teaspoon baking powder

½ teaspoon paprika

¼ teaspoon garlic salt

¼ teaspoon dried thyme

⅛ teaspoon dried rosemary

⅛ teaspoon freshly ground black pepper

2 cups corn oil, or enough to cover the chicken for frying

Rinse the chicken with cold water and pat dry with paper towels. Pour the evaporated milk into a large bowl. Add the egg and whisk to combine. In a shallow dish such as a shallow pie plate, combine the flour, salt, baking powder, paprika, garlic salt, thyme, rosemary, and pepper. Dip the chicken pieces into the milk-egg mixture and then roll in the flour-herb mixture. Set aside on a rack.

Fill a large, deep skillet halfway with the oil; there should be enough oil to cover the chicken. Heat the oil until it is very hot and registers 375°F on a deep-frying thermometer. Working in batches, fry the chicken in the oil, browning on both sides, about 15 minutes per side. Drain on paper towels and serve.

> Tip: *For frying, choose a deep heavy skillet or pot. To assure proper frying temperature, use a deep-frying thermometer. The oil will reduce in temperature as the chicken is added. Bring the oil back up to temperature between batches before adding more chicken. Maintain a temperature of at least 325°F while frying and return the temperature to 375°F between batches.*

Pauline's Easy Roast Chicken

From the kitchen of Pauline Dora Bourgeois

FAMILY FAVORITE • $ • SERVES 6

Pauline's mother, Lorraine, was married to Mike Wallace for twenty-five years. Her kitchen and healthy ways of eating rubbed off on her daughter, and here she shares with us a very simple, but delicious roasted chicken from her childhood. You should know that I am called Lorraine Two, like a boat or plane after the first Mrs. Wallace.

One 3½ to 4-pound organic free-range chicken

1 large lemon

Rinse the chicken inside and out with cold water and pat dry with paper towels. Pierce the lemon at least five times with a fork and then stuff it into the chicken's cavity. Tie the chicken legs together with kitchen twine. Place the chicken in a shallow baking dish, just large enough to hold it.

Allow the chicken to rest at room temperature, covered, for 15 minutes.

Preheat the oven to 400°F.

Roast for 15 minutes, then reduce the oven temperature to 350°F and continue to roast until golden, about 45 minutes, or until the internal temperature of the chicken registers 170°F on an instant-read thermometer when inserted into the thigh. Cut the twine and spread the legs/thigh portions away from the breasts and spoon over the pan juices. Roast for another 10 minutes. Remove from the oven and baste again. Allow to rest for 15 minutes before carving and serving on a warm platter with the pan juices.

Robin's Mediterranean Chicken

From the kitchen of Robin Jeffery

BONELESS, SKINLESS • GOOD FOR COMPANY • ONE POT • SERVES 6

Robin and her family are really good friends of ours. Robin learned to cook while living in Paris. We've enjoyed many of her delicious meals and love it when she hosts because she entertains beautifully. She and her family have since left Washington, and we're sad we don't get to see them as often. Inspired by a dish she first learned about in The Silver Palate Cookbook, this is one of her favorite recipes to make when she gathers her family of five around the table. Robin uses boneless, skinless chicken breasts, which can often dry out in some dishes, but this one stays moist since it is cooked in a savory marinade.

3 whole boneless, skinless chicken breasts (about 3 pounds)

½ cup extra-virgin olive oil

½ cup red wine vinegar

3 garlic cloves, finely minced

¼ cup dried oregano

3 bay leaves

Coarse salt and freshly ground black pepper

1 cup whole pitted prunes (8 ounces), or dried whole dates

½ cup stuffed Spanish green olives with pimientos

½ cup pitted Kalamata olives

¼ cup firmly packed dark brown sugar

½ cup freshly squeezed lemon juice

¼ cup hand-torn fresh flat-leaf parsley or cilantro

Rinse the chicken with cold water and pat dry with paper towels. Split the chicken breasts in half to make 6 pieces. Place the chicken in a large baking dish and pour over the oil and vinegar. Add garlic, oregano, bay leaves, and salt and pepper.

Turn the chicken over to coat with the marinade. Cover and refrigerate for 4 hours or overnight. Fifteen minutes prior to baking, remove the chicken from the refrigerator and let it come to room temperature, stirring again to coat with marinade. Then add the prunes and olives.

Preheat the oven to 350°F.

Just before baking, sprinkle the chicken with the brown sugar and pour the lemon juice over and around the chicken. Bake for about 30 minutes, or until the chicken is lightly browned on top and some of the liquid has reduced. Remove from the oven and discard the bay leaves.

For a family-style meal, just serve this straight from the baking dish. For a more formal presentation for guests, transfer to a large platter and spoon the prunes, capers, and olives around the chicken. Moisten with the pan juices and garnish with the fresh parsley or cilantro.

Patty's Roasted Chicken

From the Kitchen of Patty Warrender

FAMILY FAVORITE • $ • SERVES 6

Patty inherited this recipe from dear friend and chef Albertina, who spent Christmas at the Warrender's house many years ago. Albertina prepared several meals during the holidays, but her dish has evolved and become part of Patty's weekly repertoire. You can leave the carrots and peppers out, if you like, and still enjoy a delicious roasted chicken. After trying this recipe, I am sure your family will request it, too!

1 to 2 tablespoons extra-virgin olive oil

1 large Vidalia or sweet onion, cut into ⅛-inch slices

2 cups peeled and diced baby carrots or regular carrots (about 1-inch pieces)

1 large red bell pepper, seeded and very thinly sliced (optional)

4 garlic cloves, thinly sliced

2 rosemary sprigs, plus extra leaves

½ cup sherry wine

One 5-pound roasting chicken

1 teaspoon Maldon sea salt

Freshly ground black pepper

Preheat the oven to 450°F. Brush an ovenproof casserole dish evenly with olive oil.

Using three-quarters of the onion slices, cover the bottom of dish evenly. Top with 1½ cups of the carrots and the bell peppers, if using. Add slices from 2 of the garlic cloves around the sides of dish. Place the rosemary sprigs in the center of the casserole dish on top of the vegetables. Pour the sherry evenly over the ingredients in the dish.

Rinse the chicken with cold water and pat dry with paper towels. Salt the cavity of the chicken. Insert a few rosemary leaves under the breast skin. Stuff the cavity with the remaining onion, garlic, and ½ cup carrots. Place the chicken on top of the rosemary in the casserole dish. Brush the skin of the bird lightly with the oil and season with salt and pepper.

Place the casserole in the oven and roast for 30 minutes. Reduce the oven temperature to 375°F and continue roasting until done; the time will depend on the size of the bird, but usually the total cooking time is 1½ to 2 hours. Let rest for 15 minutes before carving.

Diana's Quick Chicken Divan

From the kitchen of Diana Muss

BONELESS, SKINLESS • SERVES 4

Josh Muss and I go back over decades when his wife Diana and I were raising our children in Middleburg, Virginia. We entertained, gardened, competed in show jumping and fox hunting. Yes, we did everything together with our families. This is her quick Chicken Divan recipe that Josh shares with us, which he still makes for his lady friend, Bibi, and children, Olivia and David.

3 cups water

1 chicken bouillon cube

Coarse salt

1 cup jasmine rice

2 cups broccoli florets

1½ pounds boneless, skinless chicken breasts

Freshly ground black pepper

6 tablespoons (¾ stick) unsalted butter

4 tablespoons all-purpose flour

1½ cups low-sodium chicken broth

½ cup heavy cream

2 teaspoons freshly squeezed lemon juice

Finely grated lemon zest

1 cup freshly grated Parmesan cheese

Preheat the oven to 325°F.

The basic ingredients may be prepared concurrently and combined when ready.

Rice: Bring the water to a boil. Add the bouillon cube and salt to taste. Add the rice and cook, uncovered, until the rice is firm but slightly undercooked, about 10 minutes. Drain any excess water.

Broccoli: Steam the broccoli florets until firm but slightly undercooked, about 4 minutes.

Chicken: Rinse the chicken with cold water and pat dry with paper towels. Slice the chicken breasts into ¼-inch strips crosswise. Season the chicken with salt and pepper. Melt 2 tablespoons of the butter in a skillet over medium heat. Add the chicken breasts and cook until they start to brown, then turn them over and cook on the opposite sides, about 3 minutes per side, until cooked through and an instant-read thermometer registers 170°F.

Sauce: Melt the remaining 4 tablespoons butter in a saucepan over medium heat. Add the flour slowly and whisk until thoroughly combined with the butter. Add 1¼ cups of the chicken broth to the mixture, stirring frequently, and allow to come to a boil. Reduce the heat and simmer, whisking occasionally to avoid lumps, for 15 minutes. Remove from the heat, add the cream and lemon juice and whip with a handheld electric mixer until thick, but not stiff.

Spread out the cooked rice in the bottom of an 11 × 7 × 2-inch ovenproof casserole dish. Arrange the broccoli over the rice. Pour the remaining ¼ cup chicken broth and half of the sauce over the broccoli and the rice. Arrange the chicken on top of the broccoli, sprinkle the lemon zest over the top, and pour the remaining sauce over the chicken.

Bake for 20 minutes. Remove the casserole from the oven and sprinkle the Parmesan cheese over the chicken. Return the casserole to the oven and bake until the cheese has melted, about 10 minutes more. If you prefer a crisp brown top, broil the casserole for about 2 minutes. Cut and serve with a spatula, keeping the rice and broccoli under the chicken.

Liz's Chicken Kiev

From the kitchen of Liz Dubin

FAMILY FAVORITE • BONELESS, SKINLESS • SERVES 4

My friend Liz Dubin edited a charity cookbook back in the 1970s, and one of her favorites from the book was a recipe for Chicken Kiev, which was deep-fried. I've updated it and tried to make it healthier by baking the chicken. I've added panko bread crumbs to maintain the crunchiness. Your guests—and most especially the cook—will not miss the mess of deep-frying, nor the added calories. Liz approves of the new version.

8 tablespoons (1 stick) unsalted butter, softened

2 tablespoons finely chopped fresh flat-leaf parsley

2 tablespoons finely chopped fresh chives

1 teaspoon dried tarragon

1 teaspoon ground ginger

4 boneless, skinless chicken breasts (1½ to 2 pounds total)

Make a compound butter by combining the softened butter, parsley, chives, tarragon, and ginger in a small bowl with a rubber spatula. Place a piece of plastic wrap on a flat surface and place the butter in the center of the plastic wrap. Fold over the wrap and shape the butter into a 6-inch log. Twist the ends of the plastic wrap in opposite directions to seal the log. Chill in the freezer for 15 to 20 minutes until firm.

(recipe continues on page 154)

(continued from page 153)

Coarse salt and freshly ground
    black pepper

½ cup all-purpose flour

2 large eggs, beaten

1¼ cups panko bread crumbs

Nonstick cooking spray

1 lemon cut into 6 wedges

Position a rack in the center of the oven. Preheat the oven to 350°F.

Rinse the chicken breasts with cold water and pat dry with paper towels. Remove any fat and the tender (the filet) and reserve for a another use; this will make the thickness of the breast more uniform when pounded. Place each breast between 2 pieces of plastic wrap and using the flat side of a meat mallet, pound each of the breasts to a thickness of ½ inch. Lay the breasts out on a flat work surface or cutting board and sprinkle generously with salt and pepper.

Put the flour, beaten egg, and panko bread crumbs in separate shallow dishes or pie plates. Dredge each chicken breast in the flour, dip in the beaten egg, and then coat with the bread crumbs, pressing to make the bread crumbs adhere to the chicken.

Remove the butter from the freezer and cut it into 4 pieces. Using your fingers, flatten a piece of butter into the middle of each dredged chicken breast. Roll the breasts up lengthwise and place them, seam side down, onto a baking sheet. Press in any bread crumbs that may have fallen off in the process. Spray the chicken breasts with nonstick cooking spray and bake for 15 minutes. Turn the chicken over and bake for another 15 minutes, or until golden brown. Baste each chicken breast with any butter that may have leaked out. Let rest for 10 minutes, and serve with a slice of lemon to squeeze over each.

Grace's Dad's Chicken

From the kitchen of Grace Bender

QUICK • $ • SERVES 4

Grace is a friend who is generous and full of energy—she devotes hours to worthy charitable causes and to her family. She does not like to cook, but this is her favorite chicken recipe that her father, a chef in the army, taught her many years ago. Her father prepared this dish for her family on Sunday evenings. The Bender family still enjoys this chicken weekly. Grace says to be sure to use good wine and low-sodium soy sauce.

One 3-pound chicken

2 tablespoons plus 1 teaspoon low-sodium soy sauce

2 tablespoons unsalted butter, softened

1 tablespoon coarse salt

2 teaspoons freshly ground black pepper

¼ teaspoon paprika

2 medium celery stalks, ends removed

½ cup dry white wine

Rinse the chicken with cold water and pat dry with paper towels. Let stand for 15 minutes to come to room temperature.

Position the rack to the upper-middle portion of the oven. Preheat the oven to 350°F.

Place the chicken, breast side down, in a medium roasting pan. Rub the 2 tablespoons soy sauce inside and all over the outside of the chicken. Rub the skin with the butter to coat.

Make a dry rub by combining the salt, pepper, and paprika. Rub the spices all over and under the chicken. Place each piece of celery between the wings and legs on the outside.

Combine the wine and the remaining 1 teaspoon soy sauce and pour into the bottom of the roasting pan. Bake breast side down for 25 minutes, then turn the breast side up. Baste with the pan juices; split the wings and legs from the side of the breast with a fork and, using a large spoon, pour some of the pan juices between each section. Continue to baste the chicken with the pan juices every 25 minutes, until the chicken is golden and tender, 1 to 1½ hours.

Two-By-Two Dinners

I was inspired to create this chapter by my three 20-plus-
year-old children, who are busy in the workplace and often do not have time or money to
make a nutritious dinner when they come home tired at the end of the day. Each recipe
uses two boneless, skinless chicken breasts along with a few pantry ingredients. And
since you often make two portions, it makes for good packing to take to work the next
day with your favorite salad. Just follow the instructions to make quick and easy dinners
in about 30 minutes time. Andrew, Catherine, and Sarah—work hard and eat well!!

Chicken Saltimbocca with Quick Lemon Sauce

SERVES 2

2 boneless, skinless chicken breasts (1 to 1½ pounds)

Coarse salt and freshly ground black pepper

6 fresh sage leaves

4 strips imported prosciutto

½ cup all-purpose flour

4 teaspoons extra-virgin olive oil

⅓ cup chicken broth, homemade or store-bought

Finely grated zest and juice of 1 lemon (about ¼ cup)

½ teaspoon cornstarch

Lemon wedges, for serving

Preheat the oven to 350°F.

Rinse the chicken breasts with cold water and pat dry with paper towels. Using the flat side of a meat mallet, pound each chicken breast between 2 pieces of plastic wrap to a thickness of about ¼ inch. Season with salt and pepper.

Place 3 sage leaves on each cutlet. Wrap 2 prosciutto slices around the cutlets and dredge in the flour.

In a large skillet over medium heat, warm 1 tablespoon of the oil and swirl to coat the skillet. Add the cutlets and cook for about 5 minutes on each side. Transfer to a baking sheet, place in the oven, and bake for another 10 minutes, or until cooked through.

Meanwhile, in a small bowl, combine the broth, lemon zest, lemon juice, and cornstarch and whisk until smooth. Add the cornstarch mixture and the remaining 1 teaspoon oil to the skillet. Cook, whisking constantly, until slightly thickened, about 1 minute. Return the chicken to the skillet and coat with the sauce. Serve, garnished with the lemon wedges.

Chicken Dijonnaise

SERVES 2

2 boneless, skinless chicken breasts (1 to 1½ pounds)

1 tablespoon unsalted butter

1 tablespoon extra-virgin olive oil

1 shallot, finely chopped

1 cup dry white wine

1 garlic clove, minced

¼ cup heavy cream

2 tablespoons whole-grain Dijon mustard

2 teaspoons finely chopped fresh tarragon or 1 teaspoon dried

2 teaspoons finely chopped fresh thyme or 1 teaspoon dried

Coarse salt and freshly ground black pepper

Fresh flat-leaf parsley sprigs, for garnish

Preheat the oven to 350°F.

Rinse the chicken breasts with cold water and pat dry with paper towels.

In a large ovenproof skillet over medium-high heat, melt the butter with the oil. Place the chicken breasts in the skillet and cook, turning once, until golden brown, about 4 minutes per side. Transfer to a plate and cover loosely with aluminum foil to keep them warm.

Add the shallot to the skillet and cook, stirring, until softened, about 2 minutes. Add the wine and garlic, bring to a boil, and cook until the mixture has reduced by half, about 2 minutes. Whisk in the cream, mustard, herbs, and salt and pepper to taste and bring back to a boil. Reduce the heat to medium and cook until the sauce has thickened, about 3 minutes more. Return the chicken to the skillet and coat generously with the sauce.

Transfer the skillet to the oven and bake the chicken for 15 to 20 minutes, basting once or twice with the sauce, until golden and cooked through. Garnish with the parsley and serve.

Chicken Wallace Quick Skillet Dinner

SERVES 2

2 boneless, skinless chicken breasts (1 to 1½ pounds)

2 tablespoons extra-virgin olive oil

1 garlic clove, minced

Coarse salt and freshly ground black pepper

¾ cup chicken broth, homemade or store-bought

Half of a 10-ounce bag fresh spinach, stems removed (about 2 cups)

1 cup canned cannellini beans, rinsed and drained

1 cup hand-torn fresh basil leaves

Freshly grated Parmesan cheese (optional), for serving

Rinse the chicken breasts with cold water and pat dry with paper towels.

Cut the chicken breasts into 1-inch pieces. Place in a food processor fitted with the steel blade and pulse several times until the meat is ground.

Heat the oil in a large skillet over medium-high heat. Add the garlic and cook, stirring, for about 1 minute. Add the ground chicken and season with salt and pepper. Cook the chicken until golden brown, using a wooden spoon to break up the meat as you brown it, 8 to 10 minutes.

Add the broth to the skillet and scrape up any bits from the bottom. Increase the heat, bring the mixture to a boil, and then reduce the heat and let it simmer until the liquid has reduced slightly, 10 to 12 minutes. Stir in the spinach and cannellini beans and heat through, about 2 minutes.

Remove the skillet from the heat, add the basil, and stir to combine. Serve this with Parmesan cheese, if desired.

Tip: Shorten prep time by purchasing ground chicken.

Sesame Chicken

SERVES 2

2 boneless, skinless chicken breasts (1 to 1½ pounds)

Coarse salt and freshly ground black pepper

1 teaspoon herbes de Provence

½ cup buttermilk

Nonstick cooking spray

½ cup panko bread crumbs

¼ cup plain sesame seeds, toasted

¼ cup finely chopped fresh flat-leaf parsley

2 tablespoons unsalted butter, melted

Rinse the chicken breasts with cold water and pat dry with paper towels. Put the chicken breasts on a plate large enough to hold them, and season with salt and pepper and the herbes de Provence.

Transfer the chicken breasts to a medium bowl and pour the buttermilk on top. Set aside to marinate for 15 minutes.

Position a rack in the center of the oven. Preheat the oven to 350°F. Coat a baking sheet with nonstick cooking spray.

In a small bowl, stir together the bread crumbs, toasted sesame seeds, and parsley.

Remove the chicken from the marinade and shake off the excess. One at a time, dredge the chicken breasts in the bread crumb–sesame seed mixture, coating each piece well. Season lightly with salt and pepper. Transfer the chicken to the prepared baking sheet. Discard the marinade.

Bake the chicken for about 10 minutes. Baste with the melted butter and continue baking until golden brown and cooked through, about 5 minutes more.

Chicken Fajitas

2 boneless, skinless chicken breasts (1 to 1½ pounds)

Coarse salt and freshly ground black pepper

3 tablespoons extra-virgin olive oil

2 garlic cloves, minced

Finely grated zest and juice of 1 lime

1 tablespoon chili powder

1 teaspoon dried oregano

1 large onion, halved and cut into ½-inch-thick half-moons

1 bell pepper, seeded and cut into ¼-inch-wide strips

2 jalapeño peppers, seeded and cut crosswise into rings

Warmed tortillas, for serving

Guacamole, for serving (see Anna's Secret Guacamole, page 138)

Salsa, for serving

Rinse the chicken breasts with cold water and pat dry with paper towels. Cut into ½-inch strips and season with salt and pepper.

In a large bowl, combine the chicken breast strips, 1 tablespoon of the oil, the garlic, lime zest, lime juice, chili powder, and oregano. Toss well to combine.

In a large skillet over medium heat, warm the remaining 2 tablespoons oil. Add the chicken strips and cook, turning occasionally, for about 6 minutes. Add the onion, bell pepper, and jalapeño and cook, stirring often, until the vegetables are very tender, about 5 minutes more. Serve with warmed tortillas, guacamole, and salsa and allow the diners to wrap the ingredients as desired.

Chicken Piccata

2 boneless, skinless chicken breasts (1 to 1½ pounds)

Coarse salt and freshly ground black pepper

½ cup all-purpose flour

5 tablespoons (½ stick plus 1 tablespoon) unsalted butter

3 tablespoons extra-virgin olive oil

½ cup chicken broth, homemade or store-bought

⅓ cup freshly squeezed lemon juice

¼ cup capers, drained and rinsed

⅓ cup chopped fresh flat-leaf parsley

Rinse the chicken breasts with cold water and pat dry with paper towels. Cut the chicken breasts in half horizontally. Using the flat side of a meat mallet, pound each piece between 2 pieces of plastic wrap to a thickness of ¼ inch. Season with salt and pepper. Dredge the chicken in the flour and shake off any excess.

In a large skillet over medium-high heat, melt 2 tablespoons of the butter with the oil. When the butter and oil mixture begins to foam, add the chicken and cook for about 3 minutes, or until it begins to brown. Turn the chicken over and cook the opposite sides, about 3 minutes. Transfer the chicken to a platter and cover loosely with aluminum foil to keep to warm.

Add the broth, lemon juice, and capers to the skillet and stir, scraping up the brown bits. Return the chicken to the skillet and simmer for another 5 minutes. Transfer the chicken to a serving platter.

Add the remaining 3 tablespoons butter to the pan and whisk until the sauce comes together. Stir in the parsley and cook for 2 minutes to warm through. Pour the sauce over the chicken and serve.

Herbed-Breaded Chicken Tenders with Orange Marmalade Mustard

SERVES 2

2 boneless, skinless chicken breasts (1 to 1½ pounds)

½ cup orange marmalade

¼ cup grainy Dijon mustard

2 teaspoons hot sauce

Coarse salt and freshly ground black pepper

¼ cup all-purpose flour

2 large eggs

1 cup panko bread crumbs

¼ cup chopped fresh flat-leaf parsley

½ teaspoon dried tarragon

¼ cup vegetable oil

Rinse the chicken breasts with cold water and pat dry with paper towels. Cut the chicken breasts lengthwise into long ½-inch-thick strips. In small bowl, whisk together the marmalade, mustard, hot sauce, and salt and pepper and set aside.

Place the flour in a shallow dish such as a pie plate. Beat the eggs in another shallow dish and add the panko, parsley, and tarragon to a third shallow dish. Dredge each chicken strip in the flour. Dip into the eggs, then into the bread crumbs, pressing firmly so that the bread crumbs adhere to the chicken. Set aside on a rack or a baking sheet.

In a large skillet over medium heat, warm the oil. Add the chicken strips and cook until golden brown, 3 to 5 minutes per side. Serve with the orange marmalade mustard.

Dill Havarti–Stuffed Chicken Breasts

SERVES 2

2 boneless, skinless chicken breasts (1 to 1½ pounds)

½ cup shredded dill Havarti cheese, or regular Havarti cheese and 1 teaspoon fresh or dried dill

Coarse salt and freshly ground black pepper

½ cup all-purpose flour

2 tablespoons extra-virgin olive oil

Preheat the oven to 350°F.

Rinse the chicken breasts with cold water and pat dry with paper towels. Cut a 2-inch-long pocket in the thickest part of each breast. Stuff each breast with half of the cheese. Season with salt and pepper. Put the flour in a shallow dish such as a shallow pie plate and dredge the stuffed chicken breasts in the flour.

Heat the oil in a large ovenproof skillet over medium-high heat. Add the breasts and cook until golden brown, about 4 minutes on each side. Transfer the skillet to the oven and bake the chicken breasts for about 10 minutes to finish the cooking.

Chicken and Soba Noodles One-Dish Dinner

SERVES 2

2 boneless, skinless chicken breasts (1 to 1½ pounds)

Coarse salt and freshly ground black pepper

One 8.8-ounce package soba noodles

¼ cup store-bought ginger vinaigrette

2 tablespoons canola oil

1 red bell pepper, cut into strips

4 scallions, sliced

3 tablespoons chopped cilantro

Rinse the chicken breasts with cold water and pat dry with paper towels. Using the flat side of a meat mallet, pound the chicken breasts between 2 pieces of plastic wrap into cutlets about ½ inch thick. Season with salt and pepper.

Cook the soba noodles according to the package directions, then toss with the ginger vinaigrette. Set aside.

In a skillet over medium-high heat, warm the oil. Add the cutlets and cook until golden brown, 5 to 6 minutes per side.

Transfer the cutlets to a cutting board and let cool for several minutes. When cool, slice across the grain. Toss the chicken slices, bell pepper strips, scallions, and cilantro with the dressed noodles and serve.

Chicken Cutlets alla Pizzaiola

SERVES 2

2 boneless, skinless chicken breasts (1 to 1½ pounds)

2 tablespoons extra-virgin olive oil

1 onion, thinly sliced

One 15-ounce can diced tomatoes, with their juices

2 teaspoons dried Italian seasoning

½ teaspoon crushed red pepper flakes

Coarse salt and freshly ground black pepper

2 tablespoons chopped fresh flat-leaf parsley

Rinse the chicken breasts with cold water and pat dry with paper towels.

In a large skillet over medium heat, warm the olive oil. Add the chicken breasts and cook until they are golden brown, about 4 minutes per side. Transfer the breasts to a plate and cover loosely with aluminum foil to keep them warm.

Add the onion to the skillet and cook, stirring occasionally, until soft and translucent, about 4 minutes. Add the tomatoes and their juices, the Italian seasoning, and red pepper flakes. Simmer until the flavors are blended and the juices thicken slightly, about 6 minutes. Taste the sauce and season to taste with salt and pepper. Return the chicken breasts to the skillet and coat with the sauce. Serve with the parsley sprinkled on top.

Baja Chicken with Warm Mango Salsa

SERVES 2

1 mango, peeled, seed removed, flesh diced

½ cup diced onion

½ red bell pepper, diced

¼ cup packed chopped fresh cilantro

1 jalapeño pepper, seeded and minced

2 boneless, skinless chicken breasts (1 to 1½ pounds)

1 cup all-purpose flour

1 teaspoon chili powder

½ teaspoon coarse salt

2 tablespoons unsalted butter

½ cup freshly squeezed orange juice

In a bowl, combine the diced mango, onion, bell pepper, cilantro, and jalapeño. Set the salsa aside.

Rinse the chicken breasts with cold water and pat dry with paper towels. Carefully slice each chicken breast in half horizontally and, using the flat side of a meat mallet, pound to flatten slightly. In a shallow dish such as a pie plate, combine the flour, chili powder, and salt. Dredge each chicken breast piece in the chili powder–flour mixture and set aside on a rack or baking sheet.

In a skillet over medium-high heat, melt the butter. Add the chicken and cook on each side for about 5 minutes.

Transfer the chicken to a plate. Add the mango salsa to the skillet along with the orange juice. Scrape up any bits from the bottom of the skillet and simmer until reduced slightly, about 3 minutes.

Return the chicken to the skillet and coat with the salsa. Cook to heat through, about 3 minutes. Serve the chicken on individual serving plates, topped with the salsa.

Chinese Chicken and Mushrooms

SERVES 2

2 boneless, skinless chicken
    breasts (1 to 1½ pounds)

¼ cup oyster sauce

1 tablespoon sesame oil

3 scallions, cut into 1-inch pieces

Four ½-inch pieces peeled ginger,
    cut into matchsticks

1 garlic clove, coarsely chopped

8 ounces sliced mushrooms, such
    as cremini, shiitake, or a mix

4 baby bok choy, cut crosswise
    into 1½-inch pieces (about
    1 cup)

¼ cup chicken broth, homemade
    or store-bought, mixed with
    1 tablespoon cornstarch

Cooked Chinese noodles or
    linguine, for serving

Rinse the chicken breasts with cold water and pat dry with paper towels. Cut the chicken breasts lengthwise into 2-inch-long pieces. In a bowl, toss the chicken pieces with the oyster sauce.

Heat a wok or a large, deep skillet over high heat until hot and add the oil. When the oil shimmers, add the scallions, ginger, and garlic and stir-fry for about 20 seconds. Add the chicken mixture and stir-fry until the meat is no longer pink on the outside, about 3 minutes. Stir in the mushrooms and bok choy and continue cooking for about 4 minutes more, or until the bok choy begins to soften. Add the broth-cornstarch mixture to the skillet and bring to a boil, stirring, until the chicken is cooked through and the sauce is thick and glossy, 2 to 3 minutes.

Serve the chicken and vegetables on top of a portion of the Chinese noodles or linguine.

Game Day

In this chapter, you will find great recipes for entertaining when the gang comes over to watch sporting events on TV. Many are easy to prepare ahead of time, so you can relax and enjoy the game along with your family and friends. My Mexican Chicken Casserole is a feisty one dish meal, quick to make and when served with a Southwest Chopped Salad, always a crowd-pleaser. Wings Three Ways—Sweet and Sour, Teriyaki, or Buffalo— are also simple to prepare using sauces that you create. They're generally gone before you make it back to the kitchen for seconds. If you're entertaining a smaller group, try my friend Dan's Chicken Cheeseburger Slider Salad, where you serve sliders over a bed of healthy greens.

Despite what my boys think, there are other special occasions besides the big game. In this section, I also share recipes to prepare game birds for parties and holidays that don't involve the television. Like Brined Organic Pheasant from Chef Rob Townsend at Ayrshire Farm, located in Upperville, Virginia. When I first met Rob, I was treated to a special tour of this magnificent 1,100-acre farm by its owner and founder Sandy Lerner. I also learned a lot from her farm manager John, about all the rare "heritage breeds" (see Chicken 101, page 19) of chicken and turkeys that they raise and sell.

Political guru Karl Rove shares his recipes for Two Kinds of Texas Quail, which he prepares for game dinners at his home after hunting all winter at his leasehold camp on the Armstrong Ranch in Texas. Diane Smith, wife of FedEx Corporation Founder and Chairman Fred Smith, shares her family's recipe for quail, a quick preparation, using mostly ingredients from her pantry. Diane often serves it to their wonderful family, which includes nine children and a large growing brood of grandchildren!

Alma, wife of Joe Gildenhorn, former ambassador to Switzerland, shares her recipe for Swiss Embassy Roast Turkey, which she served to embassy staff and military personnel on Thanksgiving Day in Geneva.

Goose has become a renewed popular Christmas choice for holiday meals and is readily available in many markets. I stuff my goose with fresh oranges and just toss it

opposite: Me with Larry La, owner of Meiwah restaurant, carving Peking duck.
above: Food stylist Dan Macey and me. Photo by Nancy Ellison.

top left: Chris hosting *Fox News Sunday* from the Super Bowl in Dallas, 2011, with Terry Bradshaw, Howie Long, and Michael Strahan. *top right*: Our son Rhodes Lynx pitcher Remick Smothers. Photo credit Michael Babich. *above*: Alma Gildenhorn hosting Thanksgiving Dinner at the Swiss Embassy, Geneva, Switzerland.

in the oven and let it cook. All I do is baste the bird periodically with some orange marmalade–laced syrup, and the star of my holiday meal is ready.

I have included my recipe for Smoked Orange Duck, which was inspired by the crispy duck we enjoy eating at Meiwah, our favorite Chinese restaurant in D.C. They carve it masterfully at your table while you watch—it's a great show, and Chris likes to joke that he would consider them for minor surgical procedures. Whether you're feeding the gang during halftime of the Big Game, or preparing a special holiday meal, these "Game Day" recipes are all winners.

above: Chris, Windi Grimes, Sarita Hixon, Karl Rove, and Ben Love hunting quail at the Armstrong Ranch, 2009. *below:* Me at Ayrshire Farm with the turkeys, Summer 2011.

Mexican Chicken Casserole

GOOD FOR COMPANY • VEGGIE • SERVES 8

This is a large one-dish casserole packed with Mexican spices. But, like everyone with a large family, we have a vegetarian, our daughter Megan. When she comes to visit, I prepare this dish with black beans instead of chicken. Or I prepare the casserole half with black beans and the other half with chicken.

FOR THE SALSA

Nonstick cooking spray

12 medium plum tomatoes, halved and seeded

1 small white onion, chopped

3 garlic cloves, minced

1 jalapeño pepper, seeded and quartered

⅓ cup chopped fresh cilantro

¼ cup freshly squeezed lime juice

⅛ teaspoon freshly ground black pepper

Coarse salt

FOR THE CASSEROLE

1 tablespoon corn oil

1 cup chopped onion

1 cup fresh or frozen corn kernels

1 cup diced zucchini

1 cup diced red bell pepper

2 cups shredded poached chicken breasts

1 tablespoon minced garlic

One 14-ounce can green enchilada sauce

One 4-ounce can chopped green chilies with their liquid

2 teaspoons chili powder

1 teaspoon ground cumin

Twelve 6-inch corn tortillas

1¼ cups shredded Monterey Jack cheese

Preheat the broiler to high. Coat a baking sheet with nonstick cooking spray.

To make the salsa: Combine the tomatoes, onion, garlic, and jalapeño pepper on the prepared baking sheet. Broil, turning once, for 20 minutes, or until charred. Remove from the oven and let cool slightly.

Put the charred vegetables in a food processor fitted with the steel blade. Add the cilantro, lime juice, pepper, and salt to taste. Process until smooth. Taste and adjust the seasoning, if needed, Set aside.

Preheat the oven to 350°F. Coat a 13 × 9-inch baking dish with nonstick cooking spray.

To make the casserole: In a large skillet over medium-high heat, warm the oil. Add the onion, corn, zucchini, and bell pepper and cook, stirring, until tender, about 6 minutes. Add the shredded chicken and garlic and cook, stirring, for 2 minutes more. Add the enchilada sauce, green chilies and their liquid, chili powder, and cumin and cook until heated through, about 2 minutes. Remove from the heat.

Spread 1 cup of the salsa over the bottom of the prepared baking dish. Arrange half of the tortillas over the salsa. Spread 4 cups of the chicken mixture evenly over the tortillas. Top with another 1 cup salsa. Sprinkle with ½ cup each of the cheeses. Repeat the layering, starting with the remaining tortillas and ending with the cheeses. Bake for 30 minutes until bubbly. Garnish with the chopped cilantro and serve.

1¼ cups crumbled queso fresco
cheese

½ cup chopped fresh cilantro,
for garnish

Shredded Turkey in a Bag

GOOD FOR COMPANY • POTLUCK • SERVES 8

Make this simple tangy turkey and serve it on a large platter with sesame seed buns and creamy coleslaw for a "Manwich-type" buffet for your game days! This is also fun to take for a tailgate or picnic lunch because it will not spoil in the heat.

One 5- to 6-pound turkey breast

¾ cup apple cider vinegar

1 tablespoon brown sugar

¼ cup chopped fresh flat-leaf
parsley

2 tablespoons canola oil

1 tablespoon freshly ground
black pepper

1 tablespoon coarse salt

Oven-roasting bag and tie

Coleslaw, for serving (see Vinegar
Slaw, page 212)

Sesame buns, for serving

About 15 minutes prior to baking, remove the turkey breast from the refrigerator, rinse with cold water, and pat dry with paper towels. Set on a plate, cover with aluminum foil, and allow to come to room temperature for another 15 minutes. Position a rack in the lower-middle portion of the oven. Preheat the oven to 300°F.

Combine the vinegar, brown sugar, parsley, oil, pepper, and salt in a medium bowl and whisk to combine well. Put the turkey breast in the oven-roasting bag, pour the marinade over, and secure the bag with the tie.

Put the bag with the turkey on a baking sheet and then into the oven. Bake a 5-pound turkey breast for 4 hours, or a 6-pound turkey breast for 5 hours. Remove the baking sheet from the oven and let the turkey cool in the bag for an hour.

When cool, remove the turkey breast from the bag, pour the accumulated roasting juices into a large measuring cup or fat separator and refrigerate. Using your hands or a large fork, shred the meat; discard the fat and bones. Once the juices have cooled, using a spoon, remove and discard the fat from the top. In a small saucepan, rewarm the juice and drizzle over the warm turkey meat, toss, and mound high on a large platter. Serve with the coleslaw and large sesame seed-topped buns.

Wings Three Ways

Using your pantry to create these tasty sauces for each recipe makes for an extra-special presentation. Pick one or all three of these recipes to entertain your fans. At halftime, serve the warm wings stacked high on platters with their dipping sauces on the side. Watch how quickly they disappear!

SWEET-AND-SOUR CHICKEN WINGS WITH PEANUT DIPPING SAUCE

MAKES 16 WINGS

PEANUT DIPPING SAUCE

1 cup chunky peanut butter

1 teaspoon dried ginger

1 tablespoon sesame oil

3 teaspoons soy sauce

¼ cup hot water

3 tablespoons rice wine vinegar

¼ cup freshly chopped cilantro

FOR THE WINGS

16 chicken wings (about 2 pounds)

1 cup ketchup

¼ cup Dijon mustard

¼ cup hot sauce

¼ cup soy sauce

1 tablespoon light brown sugar

Nonstick cooking spray

To make the peanut dipping sauce: Combine all the ingredients in a small bowl and mix until well combined.

To make the wings: Rinse the chicken wings with cold water and pat dry with paper towels.

In a large shallow bowl, combine the ketchup, mustard, hot sauce, soy sauce, and brown sugar and whisk to blend well. Place the wings in a large resealable plastic bag, cover with the marinade to coat evenly, and seal the bag. Refrigerate for 3 to 5 hours or overnight.

Remove the wings from the refrigerator about 15 minutes prior to cooking. Preheat the oven to 400°F. Coat a large baking sheet with nonstick cooking spray.

Remove the chicken wings from the marinade and place on the prepared baking sheet, leaving some of the marinade clinging to them. Reserve the remaining marinade for basting while baking. Bake for 15 minutes, then turn the wings over and baste with the reserved marinade. Return the wings to the oven and bake for 15 minutes more, or until cooked through. Discard the unused marinade. Serve the wings with the peanut dipping sauce.

TERIYAKI CHICKEN WINGS WITH SPICY CITRUS SAUCE

MAKES 16 WINGS

SPICY CITRUS DIPPING SAUCE

1 cup ketchup

¼ cup orange marmalade

2 tablespoons Worcestershire sauce

2 tablespoons apple cider vinegar

½ teaspoon chili powder

FOR THE WINGS

¼ cup firmly packed light brown sugar

¼ cup soy sauce

3 tablespoons unseasoned rice vinegar

1½ teaspoons cornstarch, dissolved in 1 tablespoon water

16 chicken wings (about 2 pounds)

Nonstick cooking spray

Sesame seeds

To make the spicy citrus dipping sauce: Combine the ketchup, orange marmalade, Worcestershire sauce, apple cider vinegar, and chili powder in small saucepan. Bring it to a boil and then reduce the heat to a simmer and cook for 5 minutes, until reduced.

To make the wings: In a small saucepan, combine the brown sugar, soy sauce, rice vinegar, and dissolved cornstarch and bring to a boil, whisking until the glaze has thickened, about 2 minutes.

Rinse the chicken wings with cold water and pat dry with paper towels. Place the wings in a large resealable plastic bag, cover with the marinade to coat evenly, and seal the bag. Refrigerate for 3 to 5 hours or overnight.

Remove the wings from the refrigerator 15 minutes prior to cooking. Preheat the oven to 400°F. Coat a large baking sheet with nonstick cooking spray.

Remove the chicken wings from the marinade and place on the prepared baking sheet, leaving some of the marinade clinging to them. Reserve the remaining marinade to baste while baking. Bake for 15 minutes, then turn the wings over and baste with the reserved marinade. Return the wings to the oven and bake for 15 minutes more, or until cooked through. Discard the unused marinade. Sprinkle the wings with sesame seeds. Serve with the spicy citrus dipping sauce.

BUFFALO-STYLE CHICKEN WINGS WITH LIGHT RANCH DRESSING

FAMILY FAVORITE • MAKES 16 WINGS

LIGHT RANCH DRESSING

⅔ cup buttermilk

¼ cup mayonnaise

1 tablespoon chopped fresh chives

1 tablespoon chopped fresh dill

1 tablespoon chopped fresh flat-leaf parsley

2 teaspoons Worcestershire sauce

½ teaspoon onion powder

½ teaspoon dried onion flakes

¼ teaspoon garlic powder

½ teaspoon coarse salt

¼ teaspoon freshly ground black pepper

FOR THE WINGS

5 tablespoons (½ stick plus 1 tablespoon) unsalted butter

1¼ cups Crystal Hot Sauce

16 chicken wings (about 2 pounds)

Nonstick cooking spray

Celery and carrot sticks, for serving

To make the ranch dressing: In a medium bowl, whisk together the buttermilk, mayonnaise, chives, dill, parsley, Worcestershire sauce, onion powder, onion flakes, and garlic powder. Stir in the salt and pepper. Refrigerate until needed.

To make the wings: In a small saucepan, melt the butter over medium-high heat, add the hot sauce, and stir to combine.

Rinse the chicken wings with cold water and pat dry with paper towels. Place the wings in a large resealable plastic bag, cover with the marinade to coat evenly, and seal the bag. Refrigerate for 3 to 5 hours or overnight.

Remove the wings from the refrigerator 15 minutes prior to cooking. Preheat the oven to 400°F. Coat a large baking sheet with nonstick cooking spray.

Remove the chicken wings from the marinade and place on the prepared baking sheet, leaving some of the marinade clinging to them. Reserve the remaining marinade to baste while baking. Bake for 15 minutes, then turn the wings over and baste with the reserved marinade. Return the wings to the oven and bake for 15 minutes more, or until cooked through. Discard the unused marinade. Serve with light ranch dressing and celery and carrot sticks.

Caribbean-Style Chicken

GOOD FOR COMPANY • GRILL • SERVES 6 TO 8

I call this Caribbean-style chicken because it uses all the spices from the islands. You get a great grill flavor by searing it first on the outside grill before finishing it inside in the oven. While this makes a great large game day meal, there is no reason why you can't cut the recipe in half and serve for a weeknight supper.

1 cup chopped onion

¼ cup extra-virgin olive oil, plus more for brushing

6 garlic cloves

2 teaspoons finely grated lime zest

½ cup freshly squeezed lime juice

1 teaspoon grated fresh ginger

2 tablespoons finely chopped jalapeño pepper

2 tablespoons ground allspice

2 tablespoons jalapeno pepper jelly

2 teaspoons coarse salt

2 teaspoons coarsely ground black pepper

2 teaspoons dried thyme

1 teaspoon ground cinnamon

1 teaspoon freshly grated nutmeg

6 chicken leg portions (thighs and legs, attached), bone in

6 whole chicken breasts, each split

Fresh flat-leaf parsley sprigs, for garnish

Lime wedges, for garnish

Combine the onion, olive oil, garlic, lime zest, lime juice, ginger, jalapeño, allspice, jelly, salt, pepper, thyme, cinnamon, and nutmeg in a blender and process until well blended.

Rinse the chicken in cold water and pat dry with paper towels. Place the chicken into two large resealable plastic bags and cover with the marinade. Seal the bags and refrigerate, turning occasionally, for 2 hours or overnight.

Preheat the oven to 350°F.

Preheat a gas grill to medium-high heat (450°F–500°F) and brush the grate with oil. Remove the chicken from the bag and discard the marinade. Place the chicken on the coated grill rack and sear for 5 minutes per side to make grill marks.

Transfer the chicken to a baking sheet and bake in the oven for 30 to 45 minutes until cooked through. Transfer to a platter, sprinkle with the parsley, and garnish with the lime wedges.

Panko-Crusted, Blue Cheese–Stuffed Chicken with Buffalo Sauce

BONELESS, SKINLESS • SERVES 4

Like buffalo chicken wings? Try this boneless recipe for a nice upscale alternative to the tailgate classic and surprise your fans.

4 boneless, skinless chicken breasts (6 ounces each)

½ cup crumbled blue cheese

1 tablespoon sour cream

1 teaspoon freshly squeezed lemon juice

⅛ teaspoon freshly ground black pepper

¼ cup all-purpose flour

2 tablespoons whole milk

1 large egg, lightly beaten

2 cups panko bread crumbs

3 tablespoons plus 1½ teaspoons unsalted butter

¾ cup finely chopped, drained, bottled roasted red bell peppers

2 teaspoons water

2 teaspoons Worcestershire sauce

2 teaspoons minced garlic

4 teaspoons hot sauce

Preheat the oven to 350°F.

Rinse the chicken breasts with cold water and pat dry with paper towels.

In a small bowl, combine the blue cheese, sour cream, lemon juice, and pepper. Make a 2-inch horizontal slit through the thickest part of each chicken breast to form a pocket. Stuff about 3 tablespoons of the blue cheese mixture evenly into the pockets. Put the flour into a shallow dish such as a pie plate. In a small bowl, whisk together the milk and egg. Pour the milk-egg mixture into a second shallow dish. Put the bread crumbs into a third shallow dish. Working with one chicken breast at a time, dredge the chicken in the flour. Dip into the milk-egg mixture and shake off any excess. Then coat in the panko bread crumbs pressing firmly to help the bread crumbs adhere to the chicken.

Place a large ovenproof skillet over medium-high heat, add 3 tablespoons of the butter to the skillet and swirl until the butter melts.

Add the chicken to the skillet, and cook for 4 minutes, or until browned. Turn the chicken over, transfer the skillet to the oven, and bake the chicken for 20 minutes, or until golden.

In a small saucepan over medium heat, combine the remaining 1½ teaspoons butter, roasted red bell peppers, water, Worcestershire sauce, and garlic. Bring to a simmer and cook, stirring, until the garlic has softened. Remove from the heat and stir in the hot sauce. Serve the chicken with the sauce spooned alongside.

Chicken Teriyaki

This homemade teriyaki sauce is easy to prepare and keeps for several weeks in the refrigerator, so you can use it at another time when preparing other teriyaki dishes.

3 pounds chicken wings and drumsticks

4 whole chicken breasts, split in half (about 4 pounds)

Coarse salt and freshly ground black pepper

Nonstick cooking spray

1 cup firmly packed dark brown sugar

1 cup soy sauce

½ cup unseasoned rice vinegar

4 teaspoons cornstarch, dissolved in 6 tablespoons water

Toasted sesame seeds

Pickled Cucumbers (page 227), for serving

Asian Noodles (page 200), for serving

Preheat the oven to 350°F.

Rinse the chicken with cold water and pat dry with paper towels. Transfer to a baking sheet lined with aluminum foil. Season with salt and pepper and let stand at room temperature for about 15 minutes.

Preheat the grill to medium heat (350°F–400°F). Coat an aluminum foil–lined baking sheet with nonstick cooking spray.

In a medium bowl, combine the dark brown sugar, soy sauce, rice vinegar, and dissolved cornstarch in a small saucepan and bring to a boil. Reduce the heat to low and continue to cook, whisking, until the glaze has thickened, about 8 minutes.

Working in batches, sear the chicken, just to make the grill marks on each side, about 3 minutes. Place the seared chicken on the prepared baking sheet, then brush evenly with the teriyaki glaze. Transfer to the oven and bake for 30 minutes, or until cooked through.

Remove the chicken from the oven, sprinkle with toasted sesame seeds, cover loosely with foil, and let rest for 10 minutes. Serve on a large platter accompanied by pickled cucumbers and Asian noodles.

Karl's Two Kinds of Texas Quail

From the kitchen of Karl Rove

FAMILY FAVORITE • SERVES 4

Every year our friend Karl Rove brings home the quail he shoots at his leasehold camp on the Armstrong Ranch, located near the southern border of Texas. He works for days preparing a large feast of different kinds of quail and all the trappings for his friends. Here Karl shares with us two recipes: his Spicy Texas Quail and his Quail Leg Appetizer. "Serve with cheese grits and whatever green fits your fancy," he says.

SPICY TEXAS QUAIL

4 whole quail

Two 16-ounce jars pickled jalapeños

One 8-ounce can sliced water chestnuts, drained

4 slices uncured organic bacon

Wash the quail and pat dry with paper towels. In a large bowl, marinate the birds in the full contents of two jars of pickled jalapeños overnight.

Preheat a grill to medium heat (350°F–400°F).

Remove the quail from the jalapeño marinade. Place a jalapeño slice and a water chestnut slice on the top of each quail, then carefully wrap each quail with a piece of the bacon and secure with a toothpick. Discard the unused marinade.

Place the quail on the grill and cook for 5 minutes. Turn the quail over and cook for another 5 minutes, or until the bacon is crispy and the birds are browned. The quail meat is done when it feels firm to the touch.

QUAIL LEG APPETIZER

1 package 20 quail legs (available on the Internet through Broken Arrow Ranch)

2 cups extra-virgin olive oil

¼ cup Cavender's All Purpose Greek Seasoning (available on the Internet through Cavender)

In a large bowl, cover the quail legs with the olive oil, cover the bowl with plastic wrap, and marinate overnight in the refrigerator.

Preheat the broiler on high.

Remove the quail legs from the bowl and transfer to a baking sheet. Roll the legs in the Greek seasoning.

Broil the quail legs for 2 minutes, turn the legs over, and broil on the opposite sides for 2 to 5 minutes until browned and cooked through.

Diane's Tennessee Quail

From the Kitchen of Diane Smith

QUICK • MAKES 12 QUAIL

Diane is a fun friend whom we enjoy seeing at football games with her husband Fred and their large family. They have a farm in Tennessee that is just loaded with quail. This is her large recipe for quail, which she got from a friend of her grandmother in Arkansas thirty-one years ago. Diane likes to serve it as part of a true Southern brunch along with ham, fruit compote, cheese grits, and soufflé biscuits. Sounds delicious—I want to come to brunch, Diane!

12 whole quail

Unsalted butter, for greasing the pan

Coarse salt and freshly ground black pepper

1 medium jar apricot preserves

⅔ cup low-sodium soy sauce

2 scallions, trimmed, white and pale green parts, chopped

Position a rack in the middle portion of the oven. Preheat the oven to 350°F.

Rinse the quail and pat dry with paper towels. Place the quail in a large buttered casserole dish. Season with salt and pepper.

In a medium bowl, combine the preserves and soy sauce and then mix in the chopped scallions. Pour the mixture over the quail in the dish, cover with aluminum foil, and bake until tender, about 1 hour. Uncover and bake until golden, 10 to 15 minutes more. Remove from the oven, transfer the quail to a large platter, and serve with cheese grits and fluffy biscuits.

Ayrshire Farm's Brined Organic Pheasant

From the kitchen of Rob Townsend

FAMILY FAVORITE • SERVES 4

Chef Rob gave me this recipe when I spent a beautiful summer day visiting Ayrshire Farm in Upperville, Virginia. The chef brines the organic pheasant overnight, which tenderizes and flavors the normally tough game. Brining has become a very popular method to prepare any holiday poultry.

1 gallon water

1 cup coarse salt

½ cup sugar

1 small onion, sliced

1 bunch fresh tarragon sprigs
(about ½ cup)

1 bunch fresh thyme sprigs
(about ½ cup)

6 garlic cloves, smashed

2 lemons, halved and squeezed

3 bay leaves

1 tablespoon black peppercorns,
crushed

One 2½- to 3-pound organic
pheasant, defrosted if frozen

4 tablespoons (½ stick) unsalted
butter, softened

In a large pot, large enough to hold the pheasant, combine the water with the salt, sugar, onion, tarragon, thyme, garlic, lemons, bay leaves, and peppercorns. Bring to a boil, reduce the heat, and simmer, stirring to dissolve the salt and sugar, for about 5 minutes. Remove the pot from the heat and allow to cool to room temperature. Place the pot of brine water into the refrigerator for 2 hours to cool.

Add the pheasant to the cooled brine and weight down with a plate to keep the bird totally submerged. Return the pot with the bird to the refrigerator for 6 hours.

Preheat the oven to 375°F.

Remove the pheasant from the brine, rinse well with cold water, and pat dry with paper towels.

Rub the butter inside of the pheasant's cavity. Place the pheasant on a roasting rack in a roasting pan. Roast for 1 hour. Brush with the butter that has melted inside the cavity all around the outside of the bird. Continue roasting about 1 hour more, or until the internal temperature registers 160°F on an instant-read thermometer.

Remove the pheasant from the oven and allow to rest for at least 20 minutes before carving and serving.

Swiss Embassy Roast Turkey

From the kitchen of Alma Gildenhorn
Prepared by Amy and Johnny Paras

GOOD FOR COMPANY • SERVES 6 TO 8

On special occasions, Alma likes to serve this turkey stuffed with vegetables alongside her sweet potato soufflé. This is the turkey recipe she prepared when her husband Joe Gildenhorn was the U.S. ambassador to Switzerland. She served this to the military and staff of the embassy on Thanksgiving Day while serving the country far from home.

One 12-pound organic turkey

Coarse salt

1 teaspoon crushed dried rosemary

1 teaspoon paprika

1 teaspoon freshly ground black pepper

1 teaspoon lemon pepper seasoning

2 tablespoons canola oil

Nonstick cooking spray

3 celery stalks, cut into ¼-inch dice

1 medium green apple, cut into ¼-inch dice

1 medium yellow onion, chopped

The day prior to roasting the turkey, rinse the turkey inside and out with cold water and pat dry with paper towels. Rub the inside of the cavity with coarse salt.

In a small bowl, combine 1 teaspoon salt, the rosemary, paprika, black pepper, and lemon pepper seasoning.

Rub the turkey all over with 1 tablespoon of the oil, then rub all over with the spice mixture. Place the turkey on a baking rack sprayed with nonstick cooking spray, placed in an ovenproof dish. Cover tightly with aluminum foil and refrigerate overnight.

One hour prior to roasting the bird, remove it from the refrigerator, remove the foil, and bring to room temperature. Stuff the cavity with the celery, apple, and onion.

Position a rack in the lower portion of the oven, allowing enough space for the turkey to fit. Preheat the oven to 400°F.

Place the turkey in the oven and reduce the heat to 325°F. Roast for 3 hours, basting every 30 minutes with the remaining 1 tablespoon oil and accumulated pan juices.

Remove from the oven and allow to rest for at least 20 minutes before carving and serving.

Smoked Orange Duck

Adapted from owner and Chef Larry La of Meiwah Restaurant

SERVES 4

Chris and I love Peking duck, especially at our favorite Chinese restaurant Meiwah. But owner and Chef Larry La's duck recipe requires both a walk-in refrigerator and a smokehouse—both of which most of us don't have at home. So I've come up with this similar recipe to make duck on the gas grill.

One 6-pound duck

1 tablespoon grated orange zest

2 cups freshly squeezed orange juice

½ cup diced onion

½ cup rice wine vinegar

¼ cup firmly packed light brown sugar

2 tablespoons soy sauce

1 teaspoon peeled and minced fresh ginger

1 teaspoon Chinese five-spice powder

Apple wood chips, for the grill

Rinse the duck inside and out with cold water and pat dry with paper towels. Allow to rest for 15 minutes and place on a baking sheet.

In a small saucepan, stir together the orange zest, 1 cup of the orange juice, the onion, vinegar, brown sugar, soy sauce, ginger, and five-spice powder. Bring to a boil, then reduce the heat and simmer until the mixture begins to thicken, about 3 minutes. Set aside.

Bring a large pot of water to a boil. While the water is coming to a boil, pierce the skin of the duck with a small, sharp knife, making several small slits all over the breast side of the duck. Ducks have a layer of fat just under the skin; try not to cut into the meat, but pierce only the fat layer. Place the duck in a clean sink and slowly pour the boiling water over the pierced side of the duck; this process allows the fat to render during the cooking process.

Heat two of the burners of a gas grill to low heat (300°F–350°F). Place an aluminum pan with apple wood chips soaked in water over the heated side of the grill.

Take another aluminum baking pan and place a rack over it. Place the duck on the rack. Place on the indirect heat side of the grill. Pour the remaining 1 cup of orange juice into the pan and brush some of the sauce mixture over the duck.

Cook for 4 to 5 hours, basting every half hour with the sauce mixture and turning the duck each time. The duck is done when the internal temperature registers 165°F on an instant-read thermometer, and the skin is crispy, which means that all the fat has been rendered.

Remove the duck from the grill and allow to rest at least 20 minutes before carving.

Remick's Hot Sauce Tacos

BONELESS, SKINLESS • QUICK • SERVES 4

This is my son Remick's go-to healthy meal or snack that he especially enjoyed while at home, working on his summer internship. It seems to be his favorite at school, too, since it only takes minutes to make and has a spicy kick.

1 pound boneless, skinless chicken breasts

¼ cup Louisiana hot sauce, plus extra for serving

4 whole-wheat flour tortillas

Nonstick cooking spray

1 cup store-bought salsa fresca

1 cup shredded cheddar cheese

2 cups shredded iceberg lettuce

Rinse the chicken with cold water and pat dry with paper towels. Cut the chicken breasts lengthwise into ½-inch-thick strips.

In a large resealable plastic bag, combine the chicken strips and hot sauce, coat well, and marinate in the refrigerator for at least 2 hours or overnight.

Wrap the tortillas in aluminum foil and warm in a 250°F oven while you cook the meat.

Coat a small skillet with nonstick cooking spray and place over medium-high heat. Add the chicken strips and the sauce and cook for 10 to 15 minutes until most of the liquid has cooked off and the chicken is cooked through.

Fill each warm tortilla with several strips of chicken and top with the salsa, cheese, and lettuce. Shake on additional hot sauce, if desired.

Turkey Gobbler Sandwich

QUICK • SERVES 2

There is a sandwich shop, Humphrey's Bakery, in Martha's Vineyard where beachgoers stop and order their favorite lunch as they head to the beach. Chris and the boys love this sandwich. We now make it our official day after Thanksgiving lunch. Chris jokes that it should be our traditional meal for Turkey Day—after all it is made with everything on a traditional Thanksgiving plate.

4 slices thick whole-grain bread

2 tablespoons mayonnaise

One 12-ounce can jellied cranberry sauce

Warmed sliced cooked leftover turkey, however much you can eat

Herbed Potato Bread Stuffing (page 213), warmed

Lay 4 slices of bread on a cutting board and spread a little mayonnaise on each slice of bread. Place 1 slice of the cranberry sauce on two pieces of bread. Add the turkey and top with a heaping pile of stuffing. Top with the remaining two slices of bread. Slice the sandwich in half and serve.

Dickens' Christmas Goose

For an elegant presentation and revived popular holiday fare, try this orange syrup–basted bird. When I was first married, I remember making a Christmas goose, but didn't realize until it had roasted that it didn't serve a crowd—more like a small gathering.

One 12- to 14-pound goose

Juice of 1 lemon

2 oranges, quartered

Coarse salt and freshly ground black pepper

⅔ cup corn syrup

⅔ cup orange marmalade

⅔ cup melted unsalted butter

Herbed Potato Bread Stuffing (page 213), walnuts and pumpkin seeds replaced with chestnuts

Preheat the oven to 450°F.

Remove and discard all the innards from the goose and trim any excess fat from the tail. Rinse the goose inside and out with cold water and pat dry with paper towels. Rub the inside of the cavity with the lemon juice. Stuff the bird with the orange quarters. Truss the bird like a turkey. Rub the outside with salt and pepper.

In a small bowl, combine the corn syrup, orange marmalade, and melted butter. Place the goose on a roasting rack in a roasting pan and baste with some of the orange syrup mixture. Roast for 15 minutes.

Reduce the heat to 350°F and continue to roast for 15 minutes per pound, basting the goose every half hour with the orange syrup.

Remove the goose from the oven and let rest for at least 20 minutes. Carve and serve with the stuffing.

Dan's Chicken Cheeseburger Slider Salad

From the kitchen of Dan Macey

QUICK • SERVES 8 TO 10

My friend and food stylist, Dan Macey, likes to make what he calls protein salads, that is, grilled or roasted meats served over salad greens for a one-dish meal. He developed this recipe when friends wanted an afternoon snack before heading to u Phillies baseball game.

2 pounds ground chicken

1 packet dried French onion soup mix

¼ cup whole milk

10 slices cheddar cheese, cut into quarters

Mixed salad greens or arugula

Good-quality balsamic vinegar

Preheat the oven to 350°F.

In a large bowl, combine the ground chicken, soup mix, and milk and mix well with your hands. Form the meat mixture into about 30 small patties and place on 2 baking sheets.

Bake for 13 minutes, then add the quartered cheese slices on top of each slider. Bake for another 3 minutes. Remove from the oven and serve the sliders on a platter over a bed of greens. Drizzle the sliders and greens with the balsamic vinegar and serve.

Sides

In this chapter, I've created a host of easy recipes to accompany many of my chicken dishes that will make for a well-rounded meal. I've paired some of the sides in this chapter with a specific recipe and have noted the match in the recipe headnotes.

Since I like to cook using the freshest ingredients, the pairings often highlight the seasonality of the ingredients. Some of these recipes are our family's favorites that have been handed down to me over the years while others are newfound gems.

While I've selected these pairings, feel free to mix and match the sides with the chicken dishes you cook from this book to create your own family favorites. After all, a recipe, for me, is merely a guideline to be creative with whatever I have in the pantry or can find at the local market.

Asian Noodles

From the kitchen of Chantima Suka

$ • MAKES 8 CUPS

Remick requested the noodles from the deli section at our local market so often that Chantima decided to recreate the dish by simply tasting the noodles. Now we make and enjoy these Asian noodles as a side dish or just to eat by the forkful!

¼ cup vegetable oil

3 tablespoons toasted sesame oil

3 tablespoons soy sauce

3 tablespoons oyster sauce

2 tablespoons apple cider vinegar

1 tablespoon sugar

2 teaspoons minced garlic

2 teaspoons peeled and grated fresh ginger

2 tablespoons toasted sesame seeds

1 pound linguine

1 cup julienned carrots (about 2 large carrots)

¾ cup finely chopped fresh cilantro

¼ teaspoon crushed red pepper flakes or more if desired

Freshly ground black pepper

In a medium bowl, combine the vegetable oil, sesame oil, soy sauce, oyster sauce, vinegar, sugar, garlic, ginger, and sesame seeds and stir until the sugar dissolves.

In a large pot of boiling salted water, cook the linguine according to the package directions until al dente. Drain and rinse with cold water to cool. Transfer the noodles to a large bowl, add the sauce, and toss to coat the noodles well. Add the carrots and cilantro and toss to combine. Season with red pepper flakes and black pepper to taste.

Baked Brown Rice

QUICK • SERVES 6

Brown rice can be a real pain to cook on the stovetop, if you ask me. Instead, try tossing some rice and chicken broth into a baking dish, covering it, and popping it in the oven. Then forget about it until perfectly cooked. What could be easier?

1½ cups brown rice

2½ cups chicken broth, homemade or store-bought

1 teaspoon coarse salt

1 teaspoon freshly ground black pepper

1 teaspoon poultry seasoning

1 carrot, peeled and diced

1 celery stalk, diced

Preheat the oven to 350°F.

In an 8 × 8-inch square baking dish, stir together the rice, chicken broth, salt, pepper, and poultry seasoning. Add the carrot and celery and stir to combine.

Cover the dish with aluminum foil and bake the rice for 1 hour and 20 minutes. Fluff with a fork and serve immediately.

French Lentils

SERVES 6

The black Le Puy lentils are mildly peppery in flavor and couldn't be easier to prepare. And more importantly, Chris loves them.

1 cup black lentils, such as Le Puy

3 cups vegetable broth or chicken broth, homemade or store-bought

1 teaspoon herbes de Provence

1 garlic clove

½ teaspoon coarse salt

¼ teaspoon freshly ground black pepper

1 bay leaf

1 medium carrot, peeled and cut into small dice (about ½ cup)

In a medium saucepan over medium-high heat, combine the lentils, broth, herbes de Provence, garlic, salt, pepper, and bay leaf. Bring to a boil, then add the carrot and stir to combine. Reduce the heat to medium low so the liquid is barely bubbling, cover, and cook, stirring occasionally, until most of the liquid has been absorbed and the lentils and carrot are soft, about 30 minutes.

Discard the garlic and bay leaf. Transfer the lentils to a warm bowl and serve with roasted poultry.

Black-Eyed Pea Salad

FAMILY FAVORITE • FEEDS A CROWD

We have a Southern tradition in our household that on New Year's we eat this vegetable-loaded, black-eyed pea salad to ring in the New Year with "Good Luck." I like to serve this in large martini glasses placed between couples at the dining room table for our celebration at home.

8 cups water

3 tablespoons dried basil

1 tablespoon plus 1 teaspoon coarse salt

3 pounds fresh black-eyed peas or frozen, defrosted

2 medium sweet red bell peppers, cut into medium dice

2 medium green bell peppers, cut into medium dice

1 small red onion, chopped

1 cup chopped fresh curly parsley

⅓ cup sweet sparkling wine, such as Asti Spumante

⅓ cup rice wine vinegar

⅔ cup safflower oil

1 teaspoon freshly ground black pepper

In a large saucepan over medium-high heat, bring the water, basil, and 1 tablespoon of the salt to a boil. Reduce the heat and simmer for 5 minutes. Add the black-eyed peas and cook over medium-low heat until tender but not mushy, about 45 minutes. Drain and allow to completely cool.

In a large bowl, toss the bell peppers, onion, and parsley with the cooled black-eyed peas. In a small bowl, whisk together the champagne, vinegar, oil, the remaining teaspoon of salt, and the pepper. Pour the dressing over the salad, cover tightly, and refrigerate for 1 day. Store in the refrigerator up to five days.

Serve at room temperature.

Note: *If you make this salad in advance, be sure to bring it to room temperature an hour before serving.*

Classic Mashed Potatoes

FAMILY FAVORITE • SERVES 4

When you boil the potatoes with the skins on and then peel them, it makes them fluffier when you go to mash them with warm milk and butter. I've included some popular variations for this simple side dish that include garlic, pesto, sour cream, or just bacon and cheddar cheese so you can adapt them to suit your main course.

4 large russet potatoes
  (2 to 2½ pounds), unpeeled

4 tablespoons (½ stick)
  unsalted butter

2 teaspoons coarse salt

1 cup whole milk

Freshly ground black pepper

Place the unpeeled, whole potatoes in a large saucepan and cover with water, about 2 inches above the potatoes. Bring to a boil over high heat, then reduce the heat to medium and cook, partially covered, until the potatoes are tender when tested with a fork, 35 to 40 minutes.

Drain the potatoes in a colander and let cool in the colander until they can be handled. Carefully peel the potatoes and return them to the pot over low heat to dry out the potatoes, about 1 minute. Add the butter and salt and mash with a potato masher until crumbly. Add the milk and continue to mash until creamy and smooth. You might have to add more milk to reach your desired consistency. Taste for seasoning and add more salt and pepper, if needed.

Variations

Garlic Mashed Potatoes: Warm the milk over low heat, add 1 to 2 garlic cloves, and cook for about 5 minutes. Remove from the heat and allow to infuse. When ready to combine with your potatoes, remove the garlic with a slotted spoon, and discard.

Pesto Mashed Potatoes: Reduce the milk to 2 to 3 tablespoons, then beat in ¼ to ½ cup pesto, or to taste.

Sour Cream Mashed Potatoes: Reduce the milk to 2 to 3 tablespoons and add ½ cup sour cream and a squeeze of lemon juice. Serve the potatoes with chopped fresh chives sprinkled on top.

Cheddar and Bacon Mashed Potatoes: Fold in 1 cup grated cheddar cheese and 3 slices crumbled cooked bacon.

Classic Moroccan Couscous Salad

GOOD FOR COMPANY • SERVES 6

I love how the combination of the fruits and vegetables in this dish meld with the fragrant spices that would brighten any chicken dish. Chris enjoys this salad with his Saturday night chicken suppers. It keeps for a week in the refrigerator.

3 cups chicken broth, homemade or store-bought

1½ cup plain couscous

4½ tablespoons extra-virgin olive oil

½ tablespoon ground ginger

¼ teaspoon saffron threads

½ cup black currants or raisins

½ cup chopped pitted dates

1 cup diced celery

¾ cup peeled, diced carrots

2 teaspoons minced garlic

½ cup chopped fresh flat-leaf parsley or mint

1 tablespoon freshly squeezed lemon juice

½ teaspoon coarse salt

¼ teaspoon ground cinnamon

½ cup toasted pine nuts

In a large pot, combine the chicken broth, couscous, 2½ tablespoons of the olive oil, the ginger, and saffron and bring to a boil. Remove from the heat and fold in the currants and dates. Cover the couscous with a tight-fitting lid and let stand for 12 to 15 minutes. Add the celery, carrots, and garlic and mix to combine with the couscous.

In a small bowl, combine the parsley or mint, lemon juice, salt, cinnamon, and the remaining 2 tablespoons oil and toss well, breaking up any clumps of couscous. Place in a large serving bowl, and top with the pine nuts. This salad can be refrigerated for up to 3 days, covered tightly.

Baked Brussels Sprouts

QUICK • SERVES 6

Hard to get your family to eat Brussels sprouts? Try this recipe and they will be asking for more. I begin making these sprouts as soon as I see them in the market on their long stalks! Chris enjoys this dish and is now a Brussels sprouts fan.

2 pounds of Brussels sprouts, tough outer leaves removed, ends trimmed

3 tablespoons extra-virgin olive oil

2 tablespoons freshly squeezed lemon juice (½ lemon)

Coarse salt and freshly ground black pepper

Preheat the oven to 325°F.

Using a serrated knife, cut the Brussels sprouts lengthwise. Place the sprouts in an ovenproof dish that has a tight-fitting lid. Sprinkle with the oil and lemon juice and toss to coat well. Season with salt and pepper and toss again. Cover with the lid, and bake for 20 minutes, or until tender.

Sautéed Red Cabbage

$ • SERVES 6

Sautéed cabbage often is overlooked as a side dish. This is a sweet and savory way to use the purple cabbage for dressing up your dinner plate.

1 tablespoon unsalted butter

1 large yellow onion, peeled and shredded

1 medium head purple cabbage, finely shredded

¼ cup white vinegar

2 tablespoons brown sugar

1 bay leaf

½ teaspoon caraway seeds

In a large nonstick skillet over medium-high heat, melt the butter. Add the onion and cook, stirring, until softened, 3 to 5 minutes. Add the cabbage and cook, stirring occasionally, until wilted, 5 to 8 minutes.

Add the vinegar, brown sugar, and bay leaf, toss to combine, and heat through. Remove from the heat and toss with the caraway seeds. Cover with aluminum foil and keep warm. When ready to serve, remove and discard the bay leaf.

Corn Salad

This is a handy dish to have in the refrigerator for hot summer days when you don't want to fuss in the kitchen. It keeps for several days refrigerated.

6 ears of corn, your choice, husked and ends removed (about 4 cups)

½ cup whole milk

Coarse salt

½ cup chopped sweet red onion

½ cup chopped red bell pepper

½ cup halved cherry tomatoes

Juice of 1 lime

1 tablespoon seasoned rice vinegar

Freshly ground black pepper

½ teaspoon cayenne pepper

½ cup fresh cilantro, stems removed and finely chopped

In a large pot, cover the corn with water and add the milk and a large pinch of salt. Bring to a boil over medium-high heat, reduce the heat, cover partially, and cook until tender, 4 to 6 minutes. Drain the corn in a colander and rinse with cold water. Let cool, then cut the kernels from the ears with a sharp knife; you should have about 4 cups corn kernels.

In a medium bowl, combine the corn kernels with the onion, bell pepper, tomatoes, lime juice, vinegar, salt, black pepper, and cayenne to taste. Fold in the cilantro and mix in well. Chill for 2 hours or overnight. Bring to room temperature before serving. The salad will keep in the refrigerator for up to 3 days, tightly covered.

Creamy Cheesy Grits

$ • SERVES 6

I think the starch in grits enhances almost any chicken dish as it takes on the flavors and juices to round out the meal. I often serve the chicken right over the grits for a hearty accompaniment.

2 cups whole milk

2 cups water

1 cup coarsely ground cornmeal

Coarse salt and freshly ground black pepper

8 ounces sharp cheddar cheese, shredded

3 tablespoons unsalted butter

In a large saucepan, bring the milk and water to a boil, watching carefully as it boils to prevent the milk from boiling over. Just as the milk comes to a boil, reduce the heat and gradually whisk in the cornmeal. Season with salt and pepper to taste. Continue to cook, whisking, until well combined and the mixture begins to thicken. Partially cover to prevent the mixture from bubbling over, and cook, stirring occasionally, until thickened, about 10 minutes.

Add the cheese and stir until melted. Finish with the butter, stirring until well combined. Serve alongside or under your favorite chicken.

Easy Baked Beans

My mom makes terrific baked beans that our family enjoys with dried baby lima beans, which she soaks overnight. Here I make a simple version just using canned beans from the pantry.

3 tablespoons extra-virgin olive oil

1 medium Vidalia or other sweet onion, chopped

1 medium sweet red pepper, chopped

4 garlic cloves, minced

Five 15-ounce cans navy or Great Northern beans, rinsed and drained

3 cups tomato sauce

¾ cups firmly packed dark brown sugar

¼ cup apple cider vinegar

¼ cup molasses

2 teaspoons dry mustard

1 teaspoon ground ginger

1 teaspoon crushed red pepper flakes

4 slices bacon

Preheat the oven to 350°F. Grease a 13 × 9-inch baking dish.

Heat the oil in a large skillet over medium-high heat. Add the onion and bell pepper and cook, stirring, until softened, about 4 minutes. Add the garlic and cook for 1 minute more.

In a large bowl, combine the onion mixture with the beans, tomato sauce, brown sugar, vinegar, molasses, mustard, ginger, and red pepper flakes. Pour the mixture into the prepared baking dish and place the bacon strips across the top. Cover the dish with aluminum foil and bake for 30 minutes. Remove the foil and bake for another 25 to 30 minutes until the bacon is crisp.

Fried Okra

From the kitchen of Nancy Parrish

Nancy and Chuck Parrish are Vineyard friends of ours. They are originally from the South, so when I needed a good ole Southern recipe for okra, I knew who to go to. Nancy rarely recommends frozen okra, but in this instance it works as well as fresh.

Canola oil, for frying

1 cup medium- or fine-ground cornmeal

⅓ cup all purpose flour

½ teaspoon cayenne pepper

¼ teaspoon garlic powder

1½ cups buttermilk

1 large egg

1 pound frozen okra, defrosted, precut in ¼-inch chunks

Coarse salt and freshly ground black pepper

In a heavy pot or cast-iron skillet, heat the oil to 350°F.

In a medium bowl, mix together the cornmeal, flour, cayenne, and garlic powder. In another bowl whisk together the buttermilk and egg.

Dip the okra into the buttermilk mixture, then dredge in cornmeal-flour mixture. Carefully drop the okra into the hot oil, being careful not to crowd the pot, and fry until golden brown. Drain, sprinkle lightly with salt and pepper to taste, and serve immediately.

Vinegar Slaw

The Carolinas are known for vinegar-based slaws. I've added mayonnaise to mine to make it tangy, creamy, and less sweet, but feel free to replace the mayonnaise altogether; just increase the sugar to a full cup and use ½ cup canola oil.

1 medium cabbage, finely shredded in food processor (about 5 cups), or one 16-ounce package shredded coleslaw

1 medium Vidalia or sweet onion, cut into quarters and finely shredded in a food processor

¾ cup apple cider vinegar

¼ cup sugar

1 teaspoon dry mustard

1 teaspoon celery seed

1 tablespoon coarse salt

1 teaspoon freshly ground black pepper

¾ cup mayonnaise

Put the shredded cabbage and onion in a large bowl.

Add the vinegar, sugar, mustard, celery seed, salt, and pepper to a medium saucepan and whisk to combine. Bring to a boil and pour the hot mixture over the cabbage and onion. Set aside to cool for at least 5 minutes. When cool, fold in the mayonnaise and toss to combine.

Cover and refrigerate at least an hour prior to serving. The slaw will keep for up to 2 days in the refrigerator.

Tip: You can use green cabbage or bagged cabbage with shredded carrots for the slaw, but not red cabbage since it will turn the slaw purple.

Herbed Potato Bread Stuffing

GOOD FOR COMPANY • SERVES 6

I love this recipe because you can either make the whole thing on the stovetop, or if you want an even moister stuffing, bake it in the oven, covered, for under a half hour. You can hold it, covered, in a 200°F oven until ready to serve.

4 tablespoons (½ stick) unsalted butter

1 cup chopped onion

1 cup diced celery

1 cup peeled and diced carrots

2 teaspoons dried thyme

1 teaspoon dried sage

½ teaspoon dried marjoram

1 teaspoon coarse salt

1 teaspoon freshly ground black pepper

¼ cup white wine

½ cup chopped walnuts

¼ cup roasted pumpkin seeds (optional)

One 12-ounce bag potato bread stuffing cubes

2 cups chicken broth, homemade or store-bought

In a large skillet over medium-high heat, melt the butter. Add the onion, celery, carrots, thyme, sage, marjoram, salt, and pepper and cook, stirring occasionally to make sure the vegetables are evenly cooked, until tender, about 5 minutes. Stir in the wine and deglaze the pan. Add the nuts, seeds, and potato bread and toss well to combine. Add the chicken broth, 1 cup at a time, and stir to combine. Allow to heat through, about 5 minutes.

Serve this straight from the stovetop if you are in a hurry, or for a deeper, more complex flavor, place it in a casserole dish, cover, and bake in a 350°F oven for 20 minutes.

Gruyère Cheese au Gratin Potatoes

GOOD FOR COMPANY • SERVES 6 TO 8

What I like about this recipe is that it's easy to prepare a day ahead. Simply add the cream right before baking. I serve these rich au gratin potatoes for all of our holiday meals.

6 medium russet potatoes, peeled and very thinly sliced

2½ cups water

1½ cups whole milk

3 whole, peeled garlic cloves

Coarse salt

3 bay leaves

1 tablespoon unsalted butter, softened

Freshly ground black pepper

Freshly grated nutmeg

1 cup heavy cream

10 ounces Gruyère cheese, grated

Position a rack in the middle portion of the oven. Preheat the oven to 375°F. Butter an 8-cup gratin dish.

Put the potatoes in a large pot and cover with the water and milk. Add the garlic, salt, and bay leaves. Bring to a boil over medium-high heat, partially covered, stirring occasionally so the potatoes do not stick to the bottom of the pot. Cook until the potatoes are tender but not falling apart, 10 to 15 minutes. Drain in a colander and discard the garlic cloves and bay leaf.

Using a slotted spoon, transfer half of the potatoes to the prepared gratin dish. Sprinkle with pepper and nutmeg, then top with half the cream and half the cheese. Cover with the remaining potatoes and repeat the layering until the dish is full.

Bake until the gratin is crisp and golden on top, about 45 minutes to 1 hour. Remove from the oven, cover loosely with aluminum foil, and let rest for 10 minutes before serving.

Greek-Style Lima Beans

STOVETOP • SERVES 4

Looking for a new way to prepare your frozen lima beans? Give them a Greek twist and serve them on a wintery day.

One 10-ounce bag frozen lima beans

1 cup water

3 tablespoons extra-virgin olive oil

2 tablespoons chopped fresh flat-leaf parsley, plus extra for garnish

1 tablespoon garlic, minced

½ teaspoon coarse salt

In a pot over medium-high heat, combine the lima beans, water, olive oil, parsley, garlic, and salt and cook for 17 to 20 minutes. Taste and add more salt, if needed. Do not drain when serving. Garnish with parsley.

Grilled Romaine Salad with Creamy Ranch Dressing

GRILL • SERVES 6

When I grill, this is a delicious way to prepare your salad while cooking outdoors. Place these romaine halves on a large platter, drizzle with ranch dressing, and top with croutons and shaved Parmesan cheese. To make your own croutons, simply cut some stale bread into cubes, toss with some olive oil and salt and pepper, and pop them into your toaster oven for a couple of minutes.

3 heads romaine lettuce, halved lengthwise

Extra-virgin olive oil, for brushing

Coarse salt and freshly ground black pepper

1 cup Light Ranch Dressing (page 183)

½ cup shaved Parmesan cheese

1 cup croutons, toasted

Preheat the grill to medium-high heat (450°F–500°F).

Brush the romaine halves with the olive oil on the cut side only. Sprinkle with a pinch of salt and pepper. Grill the romaine halves, cut side down, until slightly blackened, about 4 minutes.

Transfer to a serving platter and drizzle ranch dressing over the top and garnish with the cheese and toasted croutons.

Grilled Tomatoes

$ • GRILL • SERVES 6 TO 8

These basil-topped tomatoes are a good side dish for chicken or other meats and easy to prepare while the grill is hot and your main dish is resting and waiting to be carved.

4 medium ripe tomatoes, halved crosswise

1 tablespoon extra-virgin olive oil

½ cup chopped fresh basil

Coarse salt and freshly ground black pepper

Preheat a gas grill to low heat (300°F–350°F).

Place the tomatoes in a grill pan and lightly brush with the olive oil. Cook in the grill pan in the center of the grill until soft and nicely marked with grill marks, 2 to 3 minutes per side. Transfer to a platter and sprinkle with the basil, salt, and pepper.

Jasmine Rice

STOVETOP • SERVES 4

White rice can be so boring and tasteless. That's why I just love the nutty fragrance of jasmine rice. It can jazz up almost any ordinary dish and is such a great pairing with nearly any chicken recipe.

1 tablespoon unsalted butter

1 small onion, finely diced

1 cup jasmine rice

1½ cups chicken broth, homemade or store-bought

Coarse salt and freshly ground black pepper

In a saucepan over medium heat, melt the butter. Add the onion and cook, stirring, until the onion is translucent, about 4 minutes. Add the rice and toss with the onions.

Add the chicken broth and salt and pepper and bring to a boil. Reduce the heat and simmer, covered, for 10 minutes. Remove the lid and check for doneness. If all the broth has not been absorbed, continue to cook uncovered.

Individual Corn Puddings

FAMILY FAVORITE • MAKES 12 PORTIONS

This is another of my friend Liz Dubin's recipes from A Tasteful Collection cookbook she contributed to over thirty years ago for the Women's Auxiliary for the Hebrew Home to raise funds. I've taken it further by incorporating the chilies and topping the pudding with panko bread crumbs and Parmesan cheese.

Nonstick cooking spray

4 tablespoons (½ stick) unsalted butter

¼ cup all-purpose flour

2 teaspoons sugar

¼ teaspoon coarse salt

1¾ cups whole milk

3 cups fresh or canned corn kernels

3 large eggs, separated

Preheat the oven to 350°F. Lightly coat a 12-cup muffin pan with nonstick cooking spray.

Melt the butter in a medium saucepan over low heat. Using a whisk, stir in the flour and cook the mixture, about 2 minutes. Add the sugar and salt and continuously whisk until thickened. Slowly add the milk, a little bit at a time, and mix until smooth, whisking out any lumps, and continue whisking and cooking until bubbling and thick. Stir in the corn and cook until heated through, about 2 minutes more. Remove from the heat and stir in the egg yolks. Beat the egg whites and add to combine.

Fill the muffin cups almost to the tops with the corn mixture. Place the muffin pan on a larger baking pan with high sides. Fill the baking pan with warm water to reach halfway up the sides of the muffin cups. Bake the puddings for about 40 minutes, until the tops are golden and a toothpick inserted in the centers comes out clean.

Kale Crisps

I promise this will be one of your new favorites! I like to scatter two or three small bowls filled with these crispy vegetarian delights on the table. It's like eating potato chips—only healthier.

1 large bunch of kale, stems removed

1 tablespoon extra-virgin olive oil

Coarse salt and freshly ground black pepper

Preheat the oven to 300°F. Line two baking sheets with parchment paper.

Tear the leaves off of the center rib of the kale and tear into large pieces. Rinse the kale pieces with cold water and thoroughly dry with paper towels. (Feel free to let these stand at room temperature for up to an hour to assure they are thoroughly dry). Place in a large bowl, drizzle with the oil, and toss until completely coated.

Arrange the kale in a single layer on the lined baking sheets and sprinkle with salt and pepper. Place in the oven and bake for 15 to 18 minutes, or until crisp. Transfer to a bowl and serve.

Note: *Be sure to place the kale in one single layer on the baking sheet. Overcrowding will steam the kale rather than crisp it.*

Lemon Orzo

Orzo, because of its small size, is one of those pastas that brings out the flavors of the rest of the dish's ingredients especially well. I really like the fresh, light citrus tones of this recipe.

1 cup orzo pasta

1 tablespoon extra-virgin olive oil

Coarse salt and freshly ground black pepper

½ cup finely chopped fresh flat-leaf parsley

Finely grated zest of 2 large lemons

Cook the orzo in a pot of boiling salted water according to the package directions until al dente, 8 to 10 minutes. Drain the orzo well but do not rinse. Transfer to a serving bowl.

Drizzle with the oil and season with salt and pepper. Add the parsley and lemon zest and toss to combine.

Mushy Peas

You really need fresh mint to make this dish pop. It is a classic dish served in England at pubs along with fish and chips.

1 cup fresh flat-leaf parsley leaves

1 cup packed fresh mint leaves

3 cups fresh shelled peas or frozen and defrosted organic peas, patted dry

1 tablespoon extra-virgin olive oil

1 tablespoon unsalted butter

2 large shallots, finely chopped

2 cups chicken broth, homemade or store-bought

Coarse salt and freshly ground black pepper

Place the parsley and mint in a food processor fitted with the steel blade and pulse until finely chopped, then scrape into a bowl. Return the base to the processor without rinsing, add the peas, and pulse until very finely chopped.

Heat the olive oil and butter in a medium saucepan over medium heat. Add the shallots and cook, stirring, until softened, about 5 minutes. Add the broth and peas and bring to a simmer over medium-high heat. Cook the peas, stirring occasionally, until most of the liquid has evaporated, about 10 minutes. Season with salt and pepper to taste, then stir in the parsley-mint mixture and serve.

Panko Green Beans with Slivered Almonds

GOOD FOR COMPANY • SERVES 6

The crispy panko bread crumbs dress up this great side dish that I often serve at family buffet dinners.

2 pounds slender green beans, trimmed

½ cup slivered almonds

2 tablespoons unsalted butter

1 tablespoon extra-virgin olive oil

4 shallots, thinly sliced

¾ cup panko bread crumbs

Coarse salt and freshly ground black pepper

2 tablespoons chopped fresh flat-leaf parsley

Bring a large pot of lightly salted water to a boil over high heat. Add the green beans and cook until tender, about 5 minutes. Drain in a colander, rinse the beans under cold water, and pat dry with paper towels.

In a large skillet over medium-high heat, toast the almonds, stirring continuously, until golden brown, about 3 minutes. Transfer to a plate. In the same skillet over medium-high heat, melt the butter with the oil. Add the shallots and cook, stirring, until translucent and beginning to brown, 4 to 5 minutes.

Increase the heat to medium-high, stir in the beans, and cook until heated through and beginning to brown, about 2 minutes. Add the bread crumbs and continue to cook for another 3 to 4 minutes. Season with salt and pepper, then stir in the parsley and toasted almonds. Transfer to a warm serving bowl and serve immediately.

Note: *The blanched beans can be prepared 1 day in advance and refrigerated, covered tightly, or in a resealable plastic bag.*

Pan-Roasted Herbed Fingerling Potatoes

STOVETOP • SERVES 4

Make these crisp and golden potatoes on the stovetop and watch them disappear! My guys love to pick them up with their fingers and dip in chicken pan juices and pop them in their mouths.

3 tablespoons extra-virgin olive oil

1½ pounds small and medium fingerling potatoes, unpeeled

1 garlic clove, crushed

1 tablespoon finely chopped fresh rosemary or 1 teaspoon dried

1 tablespoon finely chopped fresh thyme or 1 teaspoon dried

1 teaspoon coarse salt

In a heavy medium skillet over medium-high heat, warm the oil. Add the fingerling potatoes to the skillet and toss to coat with the oil. Reduce the heat and cook, shaking the skillet occasionally to cook the potatoes evenly, for 25 minutes. Add the garlic, rosemary, thyme, and salt, cover, and cook until tender, about 10 minutes more.

Parsnip Puree

Parsnips are available all winter long, and this dish is a nice alternative to potatoes to plate with your chicken dish!

Nonstick cooking spray

6 large and small parsnips, peeled and cut into ¼-inch chunks

2 garlic cloves, smashed

1½ tablespoons extra-virgin olive oil

Coarse salt

¼ cup heavy cream

2 tablespoons unsalted butter

Pinch of freshly grated nutmeg

⅓ cup vegetable or chicken broth, homemade or store-bought

Freshly ground black pepper

Position a rack in the upper portion of the oven. Preheat the oven to 400°F. Coat a small baking sheet with nonstick cooking spray.

In a bowl, toss the parsnips with the garlic and oil. Season with salt to taste.

Place the parsnips on the prepared baking sheet in a single layer and roast until the edges are golden and caramelized, about 25 minutes; if they aren't cooking evenly, rotate the baking sheet. Remove them from the oven and set aside to cool slightly.

When cool, put the parsnips in a food processor fitted with the steel blade, along with with the heavy cream, butter, and nutmeg. Blend until coarse, adding broth to achieve a silky and smooth puree. Season with salt and pepper to taste. Transfer the puree to a bowl and cover with aluminum foil to keep it warm until ready to serve, up to 1 hour.

Pickled Cucumbers

$ • SERVES 4

These cucumbers retain a bit of a crunch while still being tangy. Feel free to add half a sliced, red onion to the mixture for a double-pickled flavor whammy.

½ cup rice wine vinegar

½ cup boiling water

3 tablespoons sugar

2 cucumbers, thinly sliced into disks

1 small Vidalia onion, thinly sliced

½ teaspoon coarse salt

5 whole peppercorns

In a bowl, whisk together the vinegar, boiling water, and sugar until the sugar has dissolved. Toss in the cucumbers, onion, salt, and peppercorns. Marinate, covered, in the refrigerator for 4 hours.

Sweet Potato Wedges

From the kitchen of Sarah Smothers

FAMILY FAVORITE • SERVES 4

My daughter Sarah loves to come up with creative dishes and cook with me in the kitchen for mother/daughter fun. These are her golden sweet potato wedges that are healthy and savory!

Nonstick cooking spray

3 medium sweet potatoes

2 tablespoons extra-virgin olive oil

1 tablespoon crumbled dried rosemary

½ teaspoon dried thyme

½ teaspoon coarse salt

Preheat the oven to 400°F. Coat a baking sheet with nonstick cooking spray.

Peel the sweet potatoes and cut them in half lengthwise, then into 1-inch wedges. In a large bowl, toss the sweet potatoes with the oil, rosemary, thyme, and salt until evenly until coated.

Spread the wedges out on the prepared baking sheet and roast, turning every 10 minutes, for 30 to 45 minutes until browned and tender.

Picnic Potato Salad

This potato salad is more like a German-style potato salad. The recipe calls for sweet pickle relish and mustard instead of mayonnaise. It keeps well in the refrigerator and packs well for picnics and family outdoor meals.

2½ pounds Yukon gold potatoes, scrubbed and halved

¼ teaspoon coarse salt

½ cup white wine vinegar

⅓ cup extra-virgin olive oil

2 tablespoons grained mustard

1 hard-boiled large egg, chopped

½ cup finely chopped celery

1 small white onion, finely chopped

2 tablespoons sweet pickle relish

2 teaspoons sweet pickle juice

4 radishes, sliced, for garnish

4 scallions, chopped, for garnish

In a medium saucepan, cover the potatoes with cold water, add the salt, and bring to a boil. Cook, stirring occasionally, until tender, 15 to 20 minutes.

While the potatoes are cooking, in a bowl, whisk together the vinegar, oil, and mustard until well combined. In another bowl, combine the egg, celery, onion, pickle relish, and pickle juice. Add the vinegar mixture and toss to coat.

Drain and rinse the potatoes briefly under cool water. While the potatoes are still warm, combine them with the dressed ingredients in the bowl. Transfer the potato salad to a large serving bowl and garnish with the radishes and scallions.

Southwest Chopped Salad

POTLUCK • GOOD FOR COMPANY • SERVES 6 TO 8

This is one of my go-to recipes for game days. I make a large first course and then when ready to feed my gang, toss this salad and enjoy the games!

FOR THE DRESSING

¼ cup freshly squeezed lime juice (about 2 limes)

¼ cup chopped fresh cilantro leaves

2 tablespoons extra-virgin olive oil

Coarse salt and freshly ground black pepper

FOR THE SALAD

1 large head romaine lettuce, cut in fine strips

One 15-ounce can black beans, drained and rinsed

One 15-ounce can yellow corn, drained

¾ cup halved cherry tomatoes

2 avocados, peeled, pitted, halved, cut into cubes, and coated with lime juice to prevent browning

1 cup cubed pepper Jack cheese

¼ cup very thinly sliced red onion

To make the dressing: In a medium bowl, combine the lime juice, cilantro, oil, and salt and pepper and mix well.

To prepare the salad: Put the romaine in a large salad bowl. Top with the black beans and corn. Surround with the halved cherry tomatoes. Sprinkle the top with the cubed avocado, cubed cheese, and onion. Toss with the dressing and serve.

Spinach and Mushroom Sauté

STOVETOP • SERVES 4

We like to eat spinach as a side dish weekly with our chicken suppers. Adding portobello mushrooms creates a heartier veggie side dish that you can also just eat on its own.

1 tablespoon unsalted butter

1 tablespoon extra-virgin olive oil

½ cup thinly sliced leeks
(white part only)

1 garlic clove, pressed

1 cup sliced portobello
mushrooms

1 teaspoon freshly squeezed
lemon juice

Coarse salt

2 cups fresh spinach

1 tablespoon heavy cream
(optional)

¼ cup vegetable broth,
homemade or store-bought

¼ cup freshly grated Parmesan
cheese

In a large sauté pan over medium heat, melt the butter with the olive oil. Add the leeks and cook, stirring, until softened, about 4 minutes. Stir in the pressed garlic. Add the sliced mushrooms, lemon juice, and a pinch of salt and stir to combine.

Stir in the spinach and cook until wilted. Add the cream, if using, and then the vegetable broth. Cook until the liquid has reduced to the desired consistency. Sprinkle with the Parmesan cheese and serve immediately.

Spinach Salad

GOOD FOR COMPANY • SERVES 10

Serve this savory spinach salad for your special holiday family gatherings in a large pedestal glass bowl. You can eliminate the bacon, if you wish, and add sliced button mushrooms to make it a totally vegetarian side. Sometimes, I use field greens, if spinach is not available.

FOR THE SHERRY VINAIGRETTE

1½ cups extra-virgin olive oil

¼ cup sherry wine vinegar

¼ cup red wine vinegar

Coarse salt and freshly ground black pepper

FOR THE SPINACH

10 cups fresh baby spinach leaves, rinsed and dried

1½ cups walnuts or pecans, toasted

6 thick slices bacon, cooked and crumbled

½ cup thinly sliced red onion rings

1 to 2 small green apples or pears, thinly sliced

½ cup blue cheese crumbles

To make the vinaigrette: In a small bowl, whisk the olive oil and both vinegars to combine. Season with salt and pepper.

To prepare the salad: Add the spinach to a large bowl and top with the toasted nuts, crumbled bacon, onion rings, apple or pear slices, and blue cheese crumbles. Toss with the sherry vinaigrette and serve.

Stuffed Tomatoes with Cucumbers and Feta

QUICK • SERVES 4

Let's be honest, sometimes I get tired of lettuce salads. So on those days, I like to make this recipe where scooped-out tomatoes also act as the perfect salad bowl.

4 beefsteak tomatoes
(about 2½ pounds)

2 Kirby cucumbers, chopped

½ cup crumbled feta cheese
(about 2 ounces)

2 tablespoons Italian vinaigrette

Coarse salt and freshly ground
black pepper

Cut off the top of each tomato. Scoop out and discard the seeds and pulp.

In a bowl, toss the cucumbers and feta with the vinaigrette. Season with salt and pepper to taste. Spoon the mixture into the tomatoes and serve.

Sweet-and-Sour Spring Carrots

GOOD FOR COMPANY • SERVES 6

These carrots are my go-to spring recipe for festive dinner parties and Easter dinner. But they also are great as a quick weeknight side dish.

2 pounds baby spring carrots,
peeled and green tops
trimmed to 1½ inches

1 tablespoon extra-virgin olive oil

Coarse salt and freshly ground
black pepper

¼ cup red wine vinegar

1½ tablespoons sugar

Position a rack in the middle portion of the oven. Preheat the oven to 425°F.

In a large bowl, toss the carrots with the oil and season with salt and pepper to taste. Transfer to a rimmed baking sheet and roast, stirring once, for 20 minutes, or until barely tender.

In a small bowl, whisk the vinegar and sugar until the sugar has dissolved. Remove the carrots from the oven. Drizzle the vinegar mixture over the carrots and shake the baking sheet to coat the carrots. Return to the oven and continue to roast the carrots until they are tender and the vinegar has evaporated, 5 to 8 minutes more.

Stuffed Tomatoes with Cucumbers and Feta

Vineyard Quinoa Salad

FAMILY FAVORITE • SERVES 6

The inspiration for creating this quinoa salad was one I tasted at the West Tisbury Farmers' Market in Martha's Vineyard at the spring-roll stand. This makes a great salad to take to a picnic because it contains no mayonnaise but is still packed with crunchy vegetables. Our son Remick, calls this quinoa salad his "stir-fried rice."

2 cups dried quinoa

2½ cups vegetable or chicken broth, homemade or store-bought

1 medium cucumber, peeled, seeded, halved, and diced (about ½ cup)

2 medium carrots, peeled and finely diced (about ½ cup)

1 cup finely diced red onion

½ cup chopped fresh flat-leaf parsley

½ cup extra-virgin olive oil

Juice of 1 medium lemon (about ¼ cup)

Coarse salt and freshly ground black pepper

Put the quinoa in a fine-mesh sieve and rinse under cold water until the water runs clear, not cloudy.

In a medium saucepan over medium-high heat, bring the chicken broth to a boil. Add the quinoa, stir, and return to a boil. Reduce the heat to low, cover, and simmer for 20 to 25 minutes; the germ ring will be visible around the pot when the quinoa is fully cooked. Uncover, fluff with a fork, and set aside to cool.

Transfer the cooled quinoa to a large bowl. Add the cucumber, carrots, red onion, parsley, olive oil, and lemon juice and toss to combine well. Season with salt and pepper to taste. Cover with plastic wrap and refrigerate until cold, for at least 1 hour or up to 3 days.

Index

Page numbers in *italics* indicate illustrations.

A

Al Tiramisu Tuscan Duck Stew, 76–77
Angel Hair Pasta, and Rosemary Sauce, Chicken with, 39
Ann's Hot Chicken Salad Pie, 136–138, *137*
Ann's Texas Fried Chicken, 147
Apples, Honey-Mustard Chicken with, 48
Art and Soul Fried Chicken, 102, *103*
Artichokes, and Fennel, Spring Chicken with, 92
Asian:
  Chicken Salad, Sharon's, 146
  Noodles, 200
Asparagus, Sugar Snap Peas, and Lemon Salad, Chicken Scallopine with, 96, *97*
Ayrshire Farm's Brined Organic Pheasant, 190

B

Bacon, and Cheddar Mashed Potatoes, 204
Baja Chicken with Warm Mango Salsa, 171
Baked:
  Brown Rice, 201
  Brussels Sprouts, 206, 207
Balsamic Butterflied Chicken with Roasted Vegetables, 72, 73
Barbecue Sauce, Carolina-Style, Basted Barbecue Chicken with, 112–114, *113*
Basted Barbecue Chicken with Carolina-Style Barbecue Sauce, 112–114, *113*
Beans, Baked, Easy, 210
Beer Can Chicken, Peter's, 144–145
Black-Eyed Pea Salad, 202, *203*
Blue Cheese, Blue Cheese–Stuffed Chicken with Buffalo Sauce, Panko-Crusted, 185

Bonnie's Curry Chicken Salad, 142, *143*
Brussels Sprouts, Baked, 206, 207
Buffalo:
  Sauce, Panko-Crusted, Blue Cheese—Stuffed Chicken, 185
  -Style Chicken Wings with Light Ranch Dressing, 182, *183*
Burgers:
  Chicken Cheeseburger Slider Salad, Dan's, 197
  Turkey, with Pimiento Spread, 74, *75*
Butterflied:
  Chicken, Balsamic, with Roasted Vegetables, 72, 73
  chicken, procedure, 25
  Grilled Chicken with Ginger-Citrus Marinade, 124, 125
Buttermilk, Herbed, Not-Fried" Chicken, 118

C

Cabbage, Red, Sautéed, 207
Caribbean-Style Chicken, 184
Carrots, Sweet-and-Sour, 232
Cashews:
  and Chicken in Lettuce Cups, 98, 99
  and Mushrooms, Braised Chicken with, Skoda's, 56–57
Chantima's Herb-Roasted Chicken with Vegetable Gravy, 65–66
Cheddar and Bacon Mashed Potatoes, 204
Cheese. See Blue Cheese; Cheddar; Feta; Gruyère Cheese; Havarti; Parmesan
Cheesy Grits, Creamy, 209
Chicken:
  with Angel Hair Pasta and Rosemary Sauce, 39

and Cashews in Lettuce Cups, 98, 99
Cutlets alla Pizzaiola, 170
Dijonnaise, 160
Enchiladas, 54, 55
Fajitas, 164, 165
Kebabs with Creamy Pesto Sauce, 128
Marengo, 38–39
pan sauce, 28
Piccata, 166
in a Pot, 78–80, 79
Quick Skillet Dinner, Wallace, 161
Saltimbocca with Quick Lemon Sauce, 158, 159
Scaloppine with Pears, 49
Scaloppine with Sugar Snap Peas, Asparagus, and Lemon Salad, 96, 97
and Soba Noodles One-Dish Dinner, 169
Stock, 28
Teriyaki, 186, 187
Tetrazzini, 51
Chicken Salad:
  Asian, Sharon's, 146
  Creamy, 117
  Curry, Bonnie's, 142, 143
  Pie, Hot, Ann's, 136–138, 137
Chili, -Citrus Cornish Hens with Lemon Sauce, 80–81
Chinese Chicken and Mushrooms, 172, 173
Citrus. See also Lemon; Orange
  -Chili Cornish Hens with Lemon Sauce, 80–81
  -Ginger Marinade, Butterflied Grilled Chicken with, 124, 125
  Sauce, Spicy, Teriyaki Chicken Wings with, 181
Classic:
  Chicken Pot Pie, 42–44, 43
  Mashed Potatoes, 204
  Moroccan Couscous Salad, 205
Coq au Vin, 63

Corn:
    Puddings, Individual, 218, 219
    Salad, 208
Cornish Hens, Citrus-Chili, with
    Lemon Sauce, 80–81
Country Chicken-and-
    Mushroom Fricassee, 52
Couscous, Salad, Moroccan,
    Classic, 205
Creamy:
    Cheesy Grits, 209
    Chicken Salad, 117
Crispy Pan-Roasted Chicken
    with Garlic-Thyme Butter,
    66, 67
Cucumbers:
    and Feta, Stuffed Tomatoes
        with, 232, 233
    Pickled, 227
Curry:
    Chicken Salad, Bonnie's, 142,
        143
    Red, Chicken with Vegetables,
        91
Cutlets, chicken, making, 24–25

D

Dan's Chicken Cheeseburger
    Slider Salad, 197
Diana's Quick Chicken Divan,
    152–153
Dicken's Christmas Goose, 196
Dill Havarti-Stuffed Chicken
    Breasts, 168
Dressing. See Ranch Dressing
Duck:
    Orange, Smoked, 192–193
    Stew, Tuscan, Al Tiramisu,
        76–77

E

Easy Baked Beans, 210
Edamame, Sesame Chicken
    with, 100
Enchiladas, Chicken, 54, 55

F

Fajita(s):
    Chicken, 164, 165
    Chicken Packets, 90–91
Farfalle, Pasta Salad, Herbed,
    Grilled Chicken and, 126
Fennel, and Artichokes, Spring
    Chicken with, 92

Feta, and Cucumbers, Stuffed
    Tomatoes with, 232, 233
French Lentils, 201
Fried Okra, 211

G

Garlic:
    Mashed Potatoes, 204
    -Thyme Butter, Crispy Pan-
        Roasted Chicken with,
        66, 67
Ginger, -Citrus Marinade,
    Butterflied Grilled Chicken
    with, 125
Goose, Christmas, Dicken's, 196
Grace's Dad's Chicken, 155
Gravy:
    Home-Style, Turkey Meat Loaf
        with, 70
    Vegetable, Herb-Roasted
        Chicken with, 65–66
Greek:
    Stuffed Chicken Breasts, 101
    -Style Lima Beans, 216
Green Bean(s):
    Panko, with Slivered Almonds,
        223
    and Turkey Stir-Fry, Quick,
        87
Grilled:
    Chicken and Herbed Farfalle
        Pasta Salad, 126
    Chicken Paillards, 127
    Pesto Chicken, 115–117, 116
    Romaine Salad with Creamy
        Ranch Dressing, 216
    Tomatoes, 217
Grits, Creamy Cheesy, 209
Gruyère Cheese au Gratin
    Potatoes, 214, 215
Guacamole, Anna's Secret,
    Newnam's Chicken Tacos
    with, 138–139

H

Half-Hour Chicken and Leek
    Stew, 64
Havarti, Dill—Stuffed Chicken
    Breasts, 168
Herb(ed), See also Rosemary;
    Sage; Thyme
    -Breaded Chicken Tenders
        with Orange Marmalade
        Mustard, 167

Buttermilk "Not-Fried"
    Chicken, 118
Fingerling Potatoes, Pan-
    Roasted, 224, 225
Potato Bread Stuffing, 213
-Roasted Chicken with
    Vegetable Gravy, 65–66
Holiday Lemon Chicken, 77
Honey-Mustard Chicken with
    Apples, 48

I

Ida's Baked Chicken, 93
Indian Butter Chicken, 82
Individual Corn Puddings, 218,
    219
Individual Winter Vegetable and
    Chicken Pot Pies, 68–69

J

Jasmine Rice, 217
Jerk Chicken, Monahan Family's,
    140, 141

K

Kale Crisps, 220, 221
Karl's Two Kinds of Texas Quail,
    188–189
Kebabs, Chicken, with Creamy
    Pesto Sauce, 128

L

Leek, and Chicken Stew, Half-
    Hour, 64
Lemon:
    Chicken, Holiday, 77
    Orzo, 222
    Sugar Snap Peas, and
        Asparagus, Chicken
        Scaloppine with, 96, 97
Lemon Sauce:
    Citrus-Chili Cornish Hens
        with, 80–81
    Quick, Chicken Saltimbocca
        with, 158, 159
    Spring Chicken Roll-Ups with,
        88
Lentils, French, 201
Lettuce, Cups, Chicken and
    Cashews in, 98, 99
Lima Beans, Greek-Style, 216
Liz's Chicken Kiev, 153–154
Low-Fat Chicken Tagine with
    Parsnip Puree, 106–107

M

Mango Salsa, Warm, Baja Chicken with, 171
Marinade, Ginger-Citrus, Butterflied Grilled Chicken with, 124, 125
Marsala, Chicken, Martin's, 35
Martin's Chicken Marsala, 35
Meatballs, Turkey, with Spaghetti Squash, 46, 47–48
Meat Loaf, Turkey, with Home-Style Gravy, 70
Mexican Chicken Casserole, 178–179
Monahan Family's Jerk Chicken, 140, 141
Mushroom(s):
    and Cashews, Braised Chicken with, Skoda's, 56–57
    and Chicken, Chinese, 172, 173
    and-Chicken Fricassee, Country, 52
    and Spinach Sauté, 230
Mushy Peas, 222
Mustard:
    -Honey, Chicken with Apples, 48
    Orange Marmalade, Herbed-Breaded Chicken Tenders with, 167

N

Nana's "No Peek" Chicken, 145, 147
Nancy's Braised Chicken in Orange Juice, 83
Newnam's Chicken Tacos with Anna's Secret Guacamole, 138–139
Noodles:
    Asian, 200
    Soba, and Chicken One-Dish Dinner, 169

O

Okra, Fried, 211
Orange:
    Juice, Nancy's Braised Chicken in, 83
    Marmalade Mustard, Herbed-Breaded Chicken Tenders with, 167
    Smoked Duck, 192–193
Orzo, Lemon, 222

Oven-Grilled Chicken with Roasted Grape Tomatoes, 119

P

Paillards:
    Grilled Chicken, 127
    making, 25
Panko:
    -Crusted, Blue Cheese—Stuffed Chicken with Buffalo Sauce, 185
    Green Beans with Slivered Almonds, 223
Pan-Roasted Herbed Fingerling Potatoes, 224, 225
Pantry Chicken Saté with Peanut Sauce, 94, 95
Parmesan, Chicken, Thin-Cut, 50
Parsnip:
    Puree, 226
    Puree, Low-Fat Chicken Tagine with, 106–107
Pasta. See also Angel Hair Pasta; Farfalle
    Rustica, Sausage, 45
    Salad, Herbed Farfalle, Grilled Chicken and, 126
Patty's Roasted Chicken, 151
Pauline's Easy Roast Chicken, 148, 149
Peanut Sauce:
    Dipping, Sweet-and-Sour Chicken Wings with, 180
    Pantry Chicken Saté with, 94, 95
Pears, Chicken Scaloppine with, 49
Peas, Mushy, 222
Pesto:
    Chicken, Grilled, 115–117, 116
    Mashed Potatoes, 204
    Sauce, Creamy, Chicken Kebabs with, 128
Peter's Beer Can Chicken, 144–145
Pheasant, Ayrshire Farm's Brined Organic, 190
Pickled Cucumbers, 227
Picnic Potato Salad, 228
Pie. See also Pot Pie
    Ann's Hot Chicken Salad, 136–138, 137

Pimiento Spread, Turkey Burgers with, 74, 75
Polenta Gratin with Turkey Bolognese, 62
Potatoes:
    au Gratin, Gruyère Cheese, 214, 215
    Fingerling, Pan-Roasted Herbed, 224, 225
    Mashed, Classic, 204
    Salad, Picnic, 228
    Sweet, Wedges, 227
Pot Pie(s):
    Chicken, Classic, 42–44, 43
    Winter Vegetable and Chicken, Individual, 68–69
Pudding(s), Corn, Individual, 218, 219

Q

Quail:
    Leg Appetizer, 189
    Tennessee, Diane's, 189
    Texas, Spicy, 188
Quiche, Chicken and Vegetable, Quick, 104, 105–106
Quick:
    Chicken and Vegetable Quiche, 104, 105–106
    Chicken Cordon Bleu, 89
    Chicken Divan, Diana's, 152–153
    Chicken Skillet Dinner, Wallace, 161
    Chicken Stir-Fry, 40, 41
    Lemon Sauce, Chicken Saltimbocca with, 158, 159
    Turkey and Green Bean Stir-Fry, 87
Quinoa Salad, Vineyard, 234, 235

R

Ranch Dressing:
    Creamy, 216
    Light, 183
Red Curry Chicken with Vegetables, 91
Remick's Hot Sauce Tacos, 193
Rice:
    Brown, Baked, 201
    Jasmine, 217

Robin's Mediterranean Chicken, 150
Romaine, Salad, Grilled, with Creamy Ranch Dressing, 216
Rosemary Sauce, Chicken with Angel Hair Pasta and, 39
Rotisserie Chicken á la King, 34

S

Sage, Chicken with Sweet Italian Sausage, Skewers of, 122, 123
Salad. *See also* Chicken Salad
Black-Eyed Pea, 202, 203
Chicken Cheeseburger Slider, Dan's, 197
Chopped, Southwest, 229
Corn, 208
Couscous, Moroccan, Classic, 205
Pasta, Herbed Farfalle, Grilled Chicken and, 126
Potato, Picnic, 228
Quinoa, Vineyard, 234, 235
Romaine, Grilled, with Creamy Ranch Dressing, 216
Spinach, 231
Salsa, Mango, Warm, Baja Chicken with, 171
Sandwich, Turkey Gobbler, 194, 195
Sausage:
Pasta Rustica, 45
Sweet Italian, Skewers of Sage Chicken with, 122, 123
Sautéed:
Chicken and Zucchini with Tarragon Pan Sauce, 114
Red Cabbage, 207
Sesame:
Chicken, 162, 163
Chicken with Edamame, 100
Sharon's Asian Chicken Salad, 146
Shredded Turkey in a Bag, 179
Skewers of Sage Chicken with Sweet Italian Sausage, 122, 123
Skoda's Braised Chicken with Mushrooms and Cashews, 56–57

Slaw, Vinegar, 212
Slider, Salad, Chicken Cheeseburger, Dan's, 197
Soba Noodles, and Chicken, One-Dish Dinner, 169
Sour Cream Mashed Potatoes, 204
Southern Oven "Unfried" Chicken, 129
Southwest Chopped Salad, 229
Spaghetti Squash, Turkey Meatballs with, 46, 47–48
Spinach:
and Mushroom Sauté, 230
Salad, 231
Spring Chicken:
with Artichokes and Fennel, 92
Roll-Ups with Lemon Sauce, 88
Stew:
Chicken and Leek, Half-Hour, 64
Duck, Tuscan, Al Tiramisu, 76–77
Stock, Chicken, 29
Stovetop:
Chicken, Summer, 120, 121
Chicken Cacciatore, 71
Stuffed Tomatoes with Cucumbers and Feta, 232, 233
Stuffing, Potato Bread, Herbed, 213
Sugar Snap Peas, Asparagus, and Lemon Salad, Chicken Scaloppine with, 96, 97
Sweet-and-Sour:
Carrots, Spring, 232
Chicken Wings with Peanut Dipping Sauce, 180
Sweet Potato Wedges, 227
Swiss Embassy Roasted Turkey, 191

T

Tacos:
Chicken, Newnam's, with Anna's Secret Guacamole, 138–139
Hot Sauce, Remick's, 193
Tandoori Roast Chicken, 36, 37
Tarragon, Pan Sauce, Sautéed Chicken and Zucchini with, 114

Teriyaki:
Chicken, 186, 187
Chicken Wings with Spicy Citrus Sauce, 181
Thin-Cut Chicken Parmesan, 50
Thyme, -Garlic Butter, Crispy Pan-Roasted Chicken with, 66, 67
Tomatoes:
Grilled, 217
Roasted Grape, Oven-Grilled Chicken with, 119
Stuffed, with Cucumbers and Feta, 232, 233
Turkey:
Bolognese, Polenta Gratin with, 62
Burgers with Pimiento Spread, 74, 75
Gobbler Sandwich, 194, 195
and Green Bean Stir-Fry, Quick, 87
Meatballs with Spaghetti Squash, 46, 47–48
Meat Loaf with Home-Style Gravy, 70
Roasted, Swiss Embassy, 191
Shredded, in a Bag, 179
Tetrazzini, 51

V

Vegetable(s):
and Chicken Quiche, Quick, 104, 105–106
Gravy, Herb-Roasted Chicken with, 65–66
Red Curry Chicken with, 91
Roasted, Balsamic Butterflied Chicken with, 72, 73
Winter, and Chicken Pot Pies, Individual, 68–69
Vinegar Slaw, 212
Vineyard Quinoa Salad, 234, 235

W–Z

Wagshal's Famous Roasted Hormone-Free Chicken, 32, 53
Wings Three Ways, 180–183
Zucchini, and Chicken, Sautéed, with Tarragon Pan Sauce, 114

Lorraine Wallace had two great passions growing up—riding horses and cooking. She became an expert in both. Moving to Middleburg, Virginia in the 1980s, she became a competitor on the amateur show-jumping circuit and won awards on her horse, Strait Man.

At the same time, she started her own extensive garden—growing vegetables, herbs, and flowers. She developed an appreciation for organic ingredients and a deep love for cooking.

In 1997, she married Chris Wallace and moved to Washington, D.C. With Chris' four children from a previous marriage and two of her own, Lorraine had her hands full bringing the two families together. Many of the key moments that helped the family bond were around the kitchen table, where Lorraine fed her extended family.

Photo by Nancy Ellison.